I0806620

Tea is for Everyone

A Chinese Tea Guide

茶

TABLE OF CONTENTS

A FEW THINGS BEFORE WE BEGIN...

Our mission for this book is very simple: we want to explore with you, dear reader, the beautiful and intricate world of Chinese teas.

Tea, in its myriad forms, is the most popular beverage in the world today (not counting water). Enjoyed by many different cultures, tea drinking is a standard pastime in countries like India, Turkey, Russia, the United Kingdom, Korea, Japan — and naturally, China.

Interestingly, although tea originated in China and the teas produced in this country are hands down some of the most complex and elegant in the world, it doesn't seem like much attention is paid to Chinese tea outside of Asia. Whether it's discussed with reverence in academic texts for tea enthusiasts or mentioned in a few nonchalant sentences in the more generic tea guides, Chinese tea is treated as a niche topic when it should really be the default genre.

Among other reasons, a very real language barrier that is notoriously difficult to cross, and the lack of coherence and standardization within the Chinese tea industry, are all factors that keep Chinese tea from being accessible. It is our goal here to change the status quo by responsibly demystifying Chinese tea for everyone.

While writing this book, we came across some unfortunate mistranslations that have endured over the years. For example, the same product that the western world refers to as black tea is, in actual fact, known as red tea in China and throughout Asia.

So we thought, why don't we just make things easier for everyone and call the drink by its proper name, red tea, instead? This renaming makes even more sense when you consider the fact that there is already another type of tea known as black tea in the Chinese tea world.

With that in mind, throughout the book we have applied what we believe are the true labels of each tea rather than stick with the conventional English translations. Whenever appropriate, we use the Putonghua pinyin name for the tea that we are referring to rather than a literal English translation (unless the literal translation has already entered into mainstream usage). For the Chinese characters that accompany the key English terms, we use traditional instead of simplified Chinese.

It might sound confusing now, but we promise that by the time you get through this book, things will be crystal clear.

BUT WHAT DO YOU MEAN BY TEA?

What exactly is tea? To set things straight from the beginning: only beverages made from the Camellia sinensis plant are classified as teas. Tea leaves are leaves that are plucked from the Camellia sinensis plant only — herbs and other plants don't count. (Sorry, chamomile, rooibos and other tisanes.)

The evergreen Camellia sinensis tea plant comes in shrub form or in tree form. Most tea plantations in China cultivate the tea shrub. Wild tea trees can still be found in some parts of China, including Yunnan province — believed to be the original birthplace of the tea tree.

And now we're all set. We hope this book can be of service to you in your tea appreciation journey!

A STORY AND SOME HISTORY

SO, WHAT'S THE ORIGIN STORY FOR TEA?

There's little dispute that tea originated in China, but the story surrounding its origins — or at least the story that the Chinese like to tell — is a bit more fantastical. And why not? A beverage of such prominence deserves a larger-than-life tale after all.

According to folklore, tea was discovered several thousand years ago by a know-it-all named Shennong (神農 **shén nóng**), who not only invented crazy useful things for his people (like agricultural equipment and the Chinese calendar), but was also the father of Traditional Chinese Medicine. Shennong might or might not have been a real figure in history, but it doesn't hurt to believe in his existence — if not his near-superhuman abilities.

One version of the tale claims that Shennong — who had a habit of putting poisonous substances in his mouth — was resting under a tree with a vessel of boiling water (as one does) when some of the tree leaves dropped into his bowl, infusing the water with its own flavors. This resulting bitter liquid helped to detoxify and stimulate Shennong — and tea as we know it was born.

Tea, first and foremost, was considered a type of medicine for the Chinese. According to the "Shennong Classic of Herbal Medicine" (神農本草經 **shén nóng běn cǎo jīng**), a book on medicinal plants allegedly written by the legendary figure, drinking tea can help in all aspects of one's life, from needing less sleep to being able to think faster and see better. Miracle herb indeed.

The Chinese character for tea, 茶 **chá**, is made up of component parts that mean "grass" (草 **cǎo**), "wood" (木 **mù**), and "human" (人 **rén**) — make of that what you will. The character is pronounced "cha" in Putonghua. In the southern Chinese Fujian dialect, it is pronounced "teh". It is the latter version that is believed to have made its way into the English vocabulary via British traders hundreds of years ago, finally giving us the word "tea" in English.

Wild tea trees in
Yunnan province

GETTING SERIOUS

In the early days, "tea" was made by mixing tea leaves with ingredients like onions, dates, and ginger. It was also consumed for its perceived health benefits rather than for enjoyment.

It wasn't until the Tang dynasty (618-907 CE) that tea consumption became a more sophisticated activity and specialized teaware was developed to accompany the refined drink. This was also when Chinese scholar Lu Yu wrote the "Tea Classic" (茶經 chá jīng) tome, reinforcing standards on how to enjoy the beverage. Lu Yu was a bit of a snob and shunned the practice of adding unnecessary ingredients to the drink — essentially, tea leaves with hot water was enough for him. And apparently people listened!

In the Song dynasty (960-1279 CE), tea-drinking and tea-making entered the realms of art and culture. Tea was no longer just a beverage, and tea-drinking became a popular pastime among the upper middle class.

Tea looked very different back then. In fact, its closest cousin today would be something like a matcha (green tea powder) from Japan. Back then, tea leaves were first pressed into cakes, then ground into a powder, and finally ferociously whisked into a bowl of frothy goodness. This entire tea ritual process was called Diancha (點茶 diǎn chá).

SPREADING THE LOVE

Tea is nowadays the most widely consumed beverage in the world, besides water. The Camellia sinensis plant, from which tea is made, is grown in over 50 countries, including China, India, Japan, Kenya, Sri Lanka, Turkey and Vietnam. You can find tea in homes and at cafes, bars and even streetside stalls. Whether you're visiting a friend in London or Hong Kong, chances are they'll both offer you tea. So how did tea make its way from China to all over the globe?

Let's take Japan for example. The country started to develop its very own complex tea culture since Chinese tea was first introduced there in the Tang dynasty. Japanese monks studying Buddhism in China decided to bring some tea seeds back home, and the country eventually invented its own methods of cultivating and processing tea.

Further afield, Europeans were first exposed to tea when they came to China during the 16th century, drawn by the country's exotic luxury goods and the lucrative trading opportunities it offered.

Portugal, which colonized Macau in China in the 1550s, became the first European country to trade with China. In 1662, Portuguese princess Catherine of Braganza married King Charles II of England. The princess happened to love drinking tea, and all of a sudden tea became a big deal among the English upper class.

Soon afterwards, the British East India Company (a proxy for the British Empire) rose to prominence, and tea leaves became a significant import from China. For comparison: In 1699, the English imported only six tons of tea; by 1799, the number had increased to 11,000 tons.

Up until this point, all of the tea had come from China. Wary of having China be its sole supplier, the Company commissioned "plant hunters" to cultivate Chinese tea plants in India in the early 19th century.

The climate in Darjeeling, India showed itself suitable for the small-leaf sinensis variety of the Camellia sinensis plant that was found in China, and the quality of the teas that were produced in Darjeeling quickly caught the western world's attention.

The state of Assam in India was also home to a robust local large-leaf assamica variety of Camellia sinensis that proved especially popular. The Company began cultivating this particular variety of tea in its other colonies, gradually spreading the practice of tea-making and tea-drinking to South India, Sri Lanka and Africa.

Fast forward to today, and tea has been transformed from a peculiar Asian specialty to the most popular beverage in the whole wide world.

THE BEVERAGE THAT CHANGED THE WORLD

It wasn't so long ago that tea was such an obsession for the world that it actually led to history-making wars.

There was the Boston Tea Party — a massive protest by American colonists against the British government's 1773 Tea Act. The Act imposed a high tax on teas sent from Britain to what were then known as the American colonies, and people were outraged. Protesters boarded trade ships at the Boston Harbor and tossed hundreds of chests of tea into the ocean.

That was a lot of money's worth of tea at the time, and the British Parliament reacted by passing even more punitive laws. The American colonists responded with even more protests, leading ultimately to the American Revolution in 1775. And we all know how that ended. It's therefore no exaggeration to say that tea was partly responsible for the birth of the United States of America!

The demand for tea in Britain also led to the Opium Wars in China, which are regarded as the starting point of modern Chinese history. In the 18th century, the British loved their Chinese teas, silks and porcelain. The Chinese, on the other hand, wanted nothing but silver from the British — and a trade deficit for the British ensued.

Looking to counter the imbalance, the British East India Company found the ultimate solution: smuggling opium into China. The highly addictive drug ensured an ever-growing demand in the country — bought with silver by the Chinese. Seeing that the illicit narcotics were starting to cripple a large percentage of the population, Chinese viceroy Lin Zexu was given the task of halting the opium trade in 1839.

After a failed appeal to Queen Victoria, Lin resorted to confiscating tens of thousands of chests full of opium in Canton (modern-day Guangzhou), the only trading hub available to foreigners at the time.

The British consequently took action and dispatched a small naval army to go on the offensive in Canton — kickstarting the first of two Opium Wars. It was an easy victory for Britain, and China was forced to sign the Treaty of Nanking, which consequently opened five Chinese ports to the world and ceded parts of the territory of Hong Kong to the British Empire.

Hong Kong was returned to China in 1997. The city's unique East-meets-West culture is in no small part due to its history as a British-controlled territory — and we have tea to thank for that.

TEA MAKING PROCESS

While we understand that the tea production process can feel a little abstract and academic, having a grasp of what happens every step of the way truly makes a difference to one's tea-drinking experience.

All teas undergo specific processing procedures that comprise of some or all of the following steps. In case you're not reading this book chronologically, please note that we are referring specifically to the production of Chinese-style teas made in mainland China and Taiwan here.

I

CULTIVATING

種茶 zhòng chá

All teas come from the Camellia sinensis tea plant. Even though all tea plants are technically called Camellia sinensis, there are many variations within the species. The tea plant can be divided into two varieties: the sinensis (小葉種 xiǎo yè zhǒng) and the assamica (大葉種 dà yè zhǒng). The assamica's defining feature is its larger-sized leaves, whereas the sinensis features smaller leaves.

While all tea leaves can be turned into any kind of tea, tea farmers usually selectively clone favorable plants by asexual reproduction, depending on the tea they specialize in. Such clones are then known as cultivars (品種 pǐn zhǒng). Jinxuan (金萱 jīn xuān), for example, is a famous cultivar with a milky aroma that is often used to make wulong and red tea (western black tea). You'll sometimes also hear the term varietal being used to describe a tea that was made from one specific cultivar or variety.

Harvesting tea leaves
Photo: Anji Jibaitea

2 HARVESTING

採茶 cǎi chá

Harvesting refers to the plucking of the leaves and buds off of the tea tree or tea shrub during peak tea season. The most coveted season for tea harvesting has traditionally been spring. In fact, there are a few terms to denote specific spring picking periods in China: from Jingzhe ("insect awakening" 驚蟄 **jīng zhé**), which starts from March 6 on the Gregorian calendar; to Qingming ("pure brightness" 清明 **qīng míng**), which starts from April 5; to Guyu ("grain rain" 穀雨 **gǔ yǔ**), which starts from April 20.

Generally speaking, tea plants can be harvested up to six or seven times a year starting from March all the way to November. The harvesting periods are designated as Buzhichun ("unaware of spring" 不知春 **bù zhī chūn**), spring, summer, autumn, winter, and Dongpian ("winter slice" 冬片 **dōng piàn**). But the exact time and number of harvests vary greatly, depending on the growing region, the altitude and the climate.

Tea plants tend to grow between 10 to 35 degrees Celsius. Tea plants at lower altitudes are subject to a longer growing season and can be harvested every 60 days or so. The higher the altitude, the colder it is and the slower the tea plants grow. This results in fewer harvests, and also a big difference in harvesting periods.

While tea plants from lower altitudes typically yield spring harvest in March, Gaoshan ("high mountain" 高山 **gāo shān**) regions may only reach favorable temperatures in May or June. That is why some Gaoshan regions yield spring tea as late as June and winter tea as early as September. The exact harvesting time largely depends on that year's weather, and some tea makers have told us that harvesting seasons have become more unstable in recent years, due to the increasingly unpredictable weather.

Tea can be harvested by hand or by machine, although hand-plucking remains the preferred method as it proves more consistent, giving tea makers more control over quality. Different tea types require different plucks, ranging from one bud, to one bud with one to several leaves.

3

WITHERING

萎凋 wěi diāo

Withering refers to the controlled wilting (攤晾 tān liàng) of the tea leaves for the purpose of water removal as well as oxidation. During this stage, the harvested tea leaves are spread out to dry before undergoing further processing. They start to oxidize, lose up to half their water content, degrade, turn limp to the touch and become more aromatic than their grassy former selves.

Withering can be done simply by laying out the leaves onto bamboo racks for natural exposure, or through more complex maneuvering like forcing the tea leaves through a heated-air trough.

For green, yellow and black (fermented) teas, the wilting stage is used mainly to remove water from the leaves rather than to promote oxidation (as in getting the leaves to turn dark and lose their grassy flavors). This technically excludes them from counting "withering" as a step.

4

CONTROLLED OXIDATION

氧化 yǎng huà

Oxidation occurs when the wilting tea leaves chemically react with the oxygen in the air, causing their cell walls to break down and causing them to turn a deep shade of red-brown. The leaves also lose their grassy flavors, become more aromatic, and feel soft to the touch. Tea makers have the ability to initiate, prolong and stop the oxidation process to suit their creative needs.

The level of oxidation that tea leaves go through determines to a certain extent what type of tea they eventually become. Green teas, on one end of the spectrum, do not go through very much oxidation, whereas red teas (western black teas) are mostly oxidized.

To have a say in the oxidation process — or what is sometimes referred to as controlled oxidation, versus the passive oxidation that occurs when a tea leaf naturally wilts — tea makers have a few tried-and-true options up their sleeves.

For instance, wulong tea makers will roll on or gently tumble the tea leaves, either by using automated machinery or by hand, in order to actively initiate oxidation in a process called make-green (做青 zuò qing). The rolling or tumbling must be done carefully in order to prevent excess damage to the tea leaves.

Meanwhile, red tea (western black tea) makers will place their tea leaves in a humid, warm environment to promote oxidation in a process

Tea leaves turn a shade of red-brown when they oxidize

known as wet-reddening (渥紅 wò hóng); and yellow tea makers use a special process known as wrap-yellowing (悶黃 mèn huáng).

Although every tea maker will have their own opinions about this process, it is believed by some tea experts and tea makers that oxidation is optimized when the tea leaves are exposed to moist and warm air anywhere between 24 to 30 degrees Celsius.

It is perhaps preferable to view controlled oxidation as a reaction that occurs during one or more stages in the tea-making process, rather than as a standalone or separate step altogether. For example, oxidation also occurs during the withering process for some types of teas.

FERMENTATION

發酵 fā xiào

Black tea (also known as fermented tea) is the only type of tea that further undergoes a fermentation process, whereby the tea leaves are chemically broken down by yeast, bacteria or other micro-organisms. In contrast to controlled oxidation, the fermentation stage is usually one of the last steps of the tea-making process. It is common in tea literature to use the terms oxidation and fermentation interchangeably, but they are two distinct and separate processes.

5

KILL-GREEN

殺青 shā qīng

Kill-green, known as Shaqing in Putonghua and sometimes referred to as "fixing", is a crucial — though not mandatory — step for many of the types of teas. Essentially, the tea leaves are heated to anywhere from 65 degrees Celsius to over 250 degrees Celsius (depending on whom you ask), above which oxidation is believed to come to a near halt, or slow enough to be negligible.

Kill-green methods range from quite manual procedures like wok-frying (炒青 chǎo qīng), where a person stands in front of a giant heated wok and tosses the leaves with their hands; to procedures like steaming (蒸青 zhēng qīng) and roasting (烘青 hōng qīng) that can be automated via machines.

Performing kill-green in a wok
Photo: Farmerleaf

A machine that automates the rolling process

6

ROLLING

揉捻 róu niǎn

Some tea makers use a rolling procedure to enhance the oxidation process (and hence, the flavors of the tea leaves) as well as to turn the leaves into various shapes for presentation purposes. Common shapes for tea leaves include strips (條型 tiáo xíng), spirals (條索 tiáo suǒ), spheres (球狀 qiú zhuàng), and half-spheres (半球狀 bàn qiú zhuàng). Narrow-shaped strips like Longjing (龍井 lóng jǐng) are flattened, while sphere-shaped leaves such as Tieguanyin (鐵觀音 tiě guān yīn) are wrapped in a bag and kneaded by hand or by machinery.

Leaves being laid out to dry
Photo: Farmerleaf

7

DRYING

乾燥 gān zào

The finished tea leaves are fully dried by air or machine to maintain their final shapes and to prevent unwanted further oxidation from taking place. For wulong and red teas, this step is often referred to as "roast-drying" (烘培 **hōng péi**) and is used not only dry the leaves, but to enhance their aroma and texture. It is highly technical and can encompass many different techniques, from charcoal-roasting to firewood-smoking.

The tea maker needs to understand the heat levels, duration and number of roasting sessions needed to achieve their desired results. For example, the roast-drying stage for Wuyishan rock tea can take up to seven months.

It's important to note that even once a tea is dried and packaged for sale, oxidation never truly stops so long as the tea leaves are exposed to oxygen. Therefore, teas that are minimally oxidized (like green tea) tend to have shorter shelf lives. The longer these teas sit around, the more oxidation that occurs, which alters their flavor profiles for the worse.

TYPES OF TEA

It is generally agreed that Chinese teas can be classified into six major categories or types. The current system is not a totally fair split, to be honest: some tea types are much more common than others, and some variants of teas might be labeled a certain type when in reality they share more similarities with another type.

In other words: everything is not as simple as it seems. But the category system is a neat and convenient way to grasp the myriad varieties of teas that are available in the world. It's a way of defining things specifically, when tea types actually fall more along a spectrum.

The mostly color-based tea categories roughly correspond to the tea's appearance once brewed. However, it is the processing steps the tea leaves undergo that determine their type, rather than their final color.

In this chapter, besides the characteristics of each type of tea, we also note their Traditional Chinese Medicine (TCM) properties.

PROCESSING METHOD

PROCESSING METHOD	GREEN TEA	WHITE TEA
WITHERING 萎凋 wěi diāo		●
MAKE-GREEN 做青 zuò qīng		
KILL-GREEN 殺青 shā qīng	●	
ROLLING 揉捻 róu niǎn	●	
WRAP-YELLOWING 悶黃 mèn huáng		
WET-REDDENING 渥紅 wò hóng		
WET-PILING 渥堆 wò duī		
DRYING* 乾燥 gān zào	●	●

*Some wulong teas undergo a further roasting (烘焙 hōng bèi) process after this stage.

FLAVOR PROFILES

Not trying to be snooty here, but it does help to have a flavor vocabulary when you're tasting a good (or terrible) tea and trying to describe what you're experiencing with your taste buds in a coherent way.

Here are some basic descriptors that will come in handy for your next tea tasting:

FLORAL FRUITY
GRASSY WOODY
NUTTY MILKY
HERBACIOUS
MEDICINAL
HUIGAN

回甘 huí gān

A common descriptor for complex teas such as wulong and Sheng Pu'er, Huigan refers to the sensation of sweetness that follows an initial bitterness. The location and duration of the bittersweet sensation should be noted. While certain teas produce a brief bittersweetness on the tongue, others can be felt at the back of one's throat for hours.

GREEN TEA

綠茶 lǜ chá

The most common type of tea in China in terms of production quantity, green tea stands out from the other tea types by being minimally oxidized — meaning the tea leaves are only left to wilt for a short period of time and never really get the chance to react with the oxygen in the air before they are kill-greened, rolled, and dried (see chapter 2). You can almost think of green tea as being the "rawest" type of tea available, or the closest to how tea leaves taste in their natural state, because of the way it is processed.

For green tea, the harvest period is a key factor in determining the price and quality of the final product. Leaves plucked during Mingqian (明前 **míng qián**) — or before Qingming Festival, usually around early April — are often considered the most premium harvest. Mingqian teas come from the very first plucks after winter and are known to be more tender and flavorful because of all the nutrients that are still stored within the plant.

Yuhou ("after rain" 雨後 **yǔ hòu**) teas, on the other hand, are considered lower grade. They are produced after Guyu ("grain rain" 穀雨 **gǔ yǔ**), from approximately mid April to early May on the Gregorian calendar. This period denotes an increase in rainfall, just before summer hits. The higher temperatures make the plants grow faster, but they also have less time to develop the nutrients that give the leaves a complex flavor profile. For higher elevation, cooler climate tea regions, this is not as important a distinction since harvesting only begins months after Qingming.

Out of the six tea types, green tea is the most studied in terms of the varieties and styles available, and comes in a wide range of appearances and flavors.

TASTE PROFILE

Green tea is bright and refreshing, often with grassy or nutty flavors and a prolonged, bittersweet aftertaste.

TCM PROPERTIES

Green tea is classified as inherently cold. It is said to be heat-reducing. It is drunk more during the day rather than in the evenings as the belief is green tea is more irritable to the stomach compared to more processed, darker-colored teas.

A tea plantation in Longjing
Photo: Fook Ming Tong

Did You Know?

Tea was hugely popular during the prosperous Tang (618-907 CE) and Song (960-1279 CE) dynasties, and most tea products back then were packaged into compressed tea bricks (團茶 tuán chá) for Imperial Tribute Teas (貢茶 gòng chá) that were given to court royals and involved intricate craftsmanship. The tea leaves were first kill-greened by steaming (蒸青 zhēng qīng), repeatedly stirred and agitated, then crushed into smaller pieces so that they became soft enough to compress. The resulting tea bricks were ground into powder which was then whisked in a bowl, for a frothy drink.

During the Ming dynasty (1368-1644 CE), founding emperor Zhu Yuanzhang shunned tea bricks for the more humble loose-leaf tea — and this in turn revolutionized the tea-making process. As tea bricks dropped in demand and loose-leaf tea (散茶 sǎn chá) became the mainstream preference, farmers realized that steaming was unnecessary, and turned to dry heat kill-green techniques such as pan-frying (炒青 chǎo qīng) and roasting (烘青 hōng qīng). This is how the modern style of green tea that many of us know and love, started to come into being.

WHITE TEA

白茶 bái chá

White tea is said to be the first type of tea to come into being, as it involves the least amount of processing. It appeared in documentation as early as the Zhou dynasty (1046-256 BCE). White tea is usually made from a bud and one to two leaves. The leaves typically have a visible layer of silvery-white fuzz on top (aka tea hair; this is a feature found mostly on young tea leaves).

There are only two steps involved in white tea-making: withering, then drying of the tea leaves. Traditionally, the leaves are either put under the sun to wither naturally or withered in the shade for better control of oxidation levels; this process takes up to three days. Once the desired oxidation levels have been achieved, the leaves are further dried under the sun or roasted dry in ovens set at low temperatures. Nowadays, it's also commonplace for both processes to take place with the help of machinery. As there is only minimal processing involved, the quality of white tea very much depends on the quality of the tea leaves. As a general rule, good-quality white tea leaves are silvery and airy in appearance.

White tea is among the few teas where aging is a desired quality. There's a saying: "One year tea, three year medicine, seven year treasure" (一年茶，三年藥，七年寶 yī nián chá, sān nián yào, qī nián bǎo). A new white tea is just tea, but aged for three years, it softens and turns sweeter, deeper, and is said to acquire more medicinal properties. A white tea that has been aged for more than seven years is treated like a treasure.

TASTE PROFILE

Since it is the most "natural" of all tea types, white tea tends to be rather light and crisp, with an aftertaste of soft, fruity sweetness.

TCM PROPERTIES

White tea is believed to be inherently cold. Drinking it is said to help to reduce heat in and detoxify the body. The aging process, however, is believed to tone down the cooling properties, making it more warming and soothing for the body.

YELLOW TEA

黄茶 huáng chá

Yellow tea is by far the least common type of Chinese tea, in terms of production variety and popularity. It is a close cousin to green tea, but there is an additional and extremely intricate wrap-yellowing process (悶黃 mèn huáng) that happens between the kill-green and drying stages, resulting in a slight oxidation of the tea leaves.

After the kill-green stage, the leaves are wrapped in cloth or paper bundles for up to three days. During this process, tea makers keep unwrapping, rewrapping and stirring the leaves. The tea leaves notably obtain a yellowish hue along the way. After the desired level of yellowing is achieved, tea makers finish off by drying the leaves.

As with many great inventions, the yellowing process was said to be accidentally discovered, by green tea makers. Tea leaves that were not properly stored, allowing humidity to seep through, subsequently became more oxidized and yellowed.

This yellowed tea turned out to be fragrant and richly textured, and tea makers sought to recreate the yellowing effect, thus developing the wrap-yellowing technique.

There's a phrase to describe yellow tea's defining features: Yellow Soup Yellow Leaves (黃湯黃葉 huáng tāng huáng yè). It's important to note that yellow teas that have not been laboriously wrap-yellowed tend to resemble green tea in color.

Nowadays, there are many self-proclaimed yellow teas on the market, but they might not have necessarily gone through the strenuous procedures described here. There are certainly more efficient and affordable ways to create yellow-colored tea, but yellow tea as it is officially designated, should be made according to the original orthodox wrap-yellowing method.

TASTE PROFILE

Yellow tea, like green tea, is fragrant and crisp. The yellowing process, however, tends to add more nutty notes and a velvety texture to the tea.

TCM PROPERTIES

Yellow tea is said to be inherently cold and have mild heat-reducing properties.

WULONG

烏龍 wū lóng

A partially oxidized tea, wulong (aka oolong, which is a misspelling) is beloved for its highly fragrant aromas. It typically has a nuanced flavor profile. Sometimes described as three parts red tea (western black tea), and seven parts green tea (三紅七綠 sān hóng qī lǜ), wulong occupies the complex middle ground between minimally oxidized green tea and highly oxidized red tea.

The secret to making good wulong lies in the intricate skills required to control the levels of oxidation that occur in the leaves. Wulong is generally considered the most complicated tea to produce. What distinguishes this tea type is a distinct processing step known as make-green (做青 zuò qīng), that involves bruising of the leaves. During this step, the leaves are repeatedly shaken, rolled, or tumbled (搖青 yáo qīng) until the edges are broken and turn slightly reddish; then placed in a warm and humid environment for oxidation to take place (晾青 liàng qīng).

The bruised leaves are then kill-greened under high heat. The rolling process that follows helps to further develop the tea's aroma. For this step, the tea leaves can be wrapped in a cloth bundle and kneaded on, eventually becoming tiny balls. Or, they can be rolled by hand into long thin strips. This process can be repeated multiple times, in between the kill-green and roast-drying stages, in order to accomplish the desired shape, aroma and flavors.

Wulong spans a wide range of oxidation and roast levels, from a lightly oxidized and roasted Taiwanese Baozhong; to a moderately oxidized and roasted Tieguanyin; to a heavily roasted Wuyi Yancha. Even within a certain tea style, tea makers are constantly experimenting with the oxidation and roasting levels.

Unlike other teas, wulong typically includes only tea leaves; buds are not needed, with the exception of Oriental Beauty. More mature and tougher tea leaves are used, as they need to go through more strenuous processing. Wulong is also the only tea type where the autumn harvest can be as desirable as the spring harvest. The drier and breezier autumnal climate provides a better tea-making environment for the tea makers to counteract the fact that higher quality tea leaves are produced in spring.

TASTE PROFILE

Wulong is beloved for its complex and wide-ranging aromas, from floral and fruity to sugary and toasty. Not only does it retain the lightness and freshness of green tea, but the partial oxidation also gives it a full body and a bittersweet aftertaste.

TCM PROPERTIES

As it is part red tea (western black tea) and part green tea, wulong is neither cooling nor warming, but somewhere in the middle. It is said to help reduce the heat in and revitalize one's body.

RED TEA

紅茶 hóng chá

Red tea is currently known as black tea in the west, which unfortunately causes a lot of confusion. There are some complex theories floating around to explain how this inaccurate English translation came to be, but honestly, it's far easier to just set the record straight instead. In short: it's called red tea in Chinese, so that's what we're calling it in English too.

Red tea is a mostly oxidized tea, making it the sweetest, most mellow tea type. It gained massive popularity in Britain after the tea-loving Portuguese Princess Catherine of Braganza (who later became Queen of England) introduced it to her people in 1662. In the 1800s, Britain managed to roughly replicate the Chinese red tea-making process on the tea plantations of its colonies, including India and Sri Lanka. Red tea was the only tea type that was produced on these plantations, and by extension for the western markets, until recent times.

An important distinction: western-style black tea is often called CTC (Crush Tear Curl) tea, which often comes pellet-shaped and packed in teabags. You get a much stronger brew with CTC tea, which can go well with milk and sugar. Red tea, on the other hand, is processed and drunk whole-leaf, without any condiment needed.

In fact, red tea probably tastes more similar to wulong tea than western-style black tea. Red tea is all about artfully achieving a high level of oxidation in the leaves. Generally, the leaves are withered, then repeatedly rolled by hand or machine until the leaves are tightly twisted and all the water has been released. The leaves are consequently placed in a humid and warm environment to promote oxidation in a process known as wet-reddening (渥紅 wò hóng). The leaves are then oven-dried.

Even though red tea was first documented in the Fujian mountain regions during the Ming dynasty (1368–1644 CE), it was never very popular among Chinese tea drinkers, since it was perceived as inferior to green tea. It wasn't until the early 2000s, with a more modernized tea market, that red tea started to be embraced by the nation.

Red tea is available in three forms: as a loose-leaf Gongfu Hongcha (工夫紅茶 gōng fū hóng chá); a smoked Xiaozhong Hongcha (小種紅茶 xiǎo zhǒng hóng chá); and a crushed-leaf Hongsuicha (紅碎茶 hóng suì chá).

TASTE PROFILE

Red tea is generally rich, heavy, and fragrant.

TCM PROPERTIES

Red tea is considered inherently warm and helps one to guard against the cold. It is best consumed during winter.

BLACK TEA

黑茶 hēi chá

Black tea (黑茶 hēi chá) — sometimes known as dark or fermented tea, and not to be confused with western black tea — stands out from the rest of the tea types by being fermented on top of being oxidized. It's important to differentiate between the two terms, since they are frequently used interchangeably, although they are meant to represent completely different things.

We define fermentation (發酵 fā xiào) in tea-making as the process under which tea leaves are chemically broken down by yeast, bacteria or other micro-organisms — this step does not necessarily require the presence of oxygen, which is in sharp contrast to the scientific definition of oxidation (氧化 yǎng huà).

After the kill-green and rolling processes, most black tea makers use a variation of the wet-piling (渥堆 wò duī) method, and sometimes a starter culture, to initiate fermentation.

With the typical wet-piling method, the tea leaves are piled into a one-meter-high layer on the ground, then covered with a piece of wet cloth for 24 hours to up to 45 days.

The wet pile needs to be removed from direct sunlight and stored at a temperature of 25 degrees Celsius or higher, as well as at a humidity level of around 85 percent. Nowadays,

TASTE PROFILE

Black tea is generally intense, complex, and tastes "aged" or slightly musty. It is much more full-bodied than white and green tea.

TCM PROPERTIES

Black tea is inherently warm and said to be mild and gentle for the body. It is generally recommended as an after-meal companion.

some tea makers use machinery to control the temperatures and humidity levels of the wet piles.

Fungus or mold can be a byproduct of the fermentation process, and depending on the type of black tea being made, the mold can either be removed from or left to grow on the final product.

Due to this tea type's relative ease of transport and storage, as well as its alleged ability to help with digestion, black tea has historically been popular with nomad groups that enjoy a high-fat diet.

FLORAL TEA

花茶 huā chá

Besides the six main types of teas, floral tea is also an important category of tea that occupies a special place in Chinese tea culture. Floral tea is typically made by mixing green tea leaves with highly fragrant flowers. Jasmine tea (茉莉香片 mò lì xiāng piàn), for instance, is a mix of tea leaves and jasmine petals. Floral teas have become an immensely popular style of tea for Chinese tea drinkers.

TASTE PROFILE

Floral teas are usually defined by their powerful floral aromas and bright and crisp base notes.

TCM PROPERTIES

It is said that floral tea is inherently cold, helps reduce heat in the body, and is milder than green tea.

POPULAR TEA STYLES

Make no mistake: We're not here to name-drop every style of Chinese tea that is available on the market. First, that's an impossible task — there are simply too many. And then, there is already plenty of academic literature out there that does exactly that.

Instead, we'll be highlighting some of the more well-known teas so that the next time you encounter them on your tea journey, you will be better informed and might even want to do more research yourself!

REMEMBER THIS

Here are some key terms that are commonly used in the names of different styles of teas, and what they mean in English:

Maojian - Fur Tips
Baihao - White Hair
Yinzhen - Silver Needle
Jinya - Golden Buds

GREEN TEA

綠茶 lü chá

Xihu Longjing

西湖龍井 xī hú lóng jǐng

ALSO KNOWN AS
Dragon Well, Longjing
WHERE IT'S FROM
Longjing village, Zhejiang (浙江 zhè jiāng)

Xihu Longjing — a green tea with flat and smooth leaves — is likely the most well-known style of Chinese tea, and the premium-quality varieties that are on the market can be very steeply priced indeed. Authentic Longjing must be grown in Zhejiang province, usually around the Xihu (West Lake) area in Longjing village, Hangzhou: Lion Peak (獅峰 shī fēng), Wengjiashan (翁家山 wēng jiā shān), Yunqi (雲棲 yún qī), Hupao (虎跑 hǔ pǎo), and Meijiawu (梅家塢 méi jiā wù). Plucking consists of one bud and two leaves. Minimal processing is required.

There are many varieties of Longjing in the market. More expensive varieties include Shifeng or "lion peak" Longjing (獅峰龍井 shī fēng lóng jǐng), Meiwu Longjing (梅塢龍井 méi wù lóng jǐng), and Xihu Longjing. If you're looking for more reasonably priced ones, try Longjing from outside the Xihu area, such as Qiantang Longjing (錢塘龍井 qián táng lóng jǐng). When making a purchase, look for glossy and smooth-surfaced tea leaves, and uniform leaf shapes and sizes. Good Longjing tea makes a light and bright brew with a refreshing flavor and a delightful hit of sweetness.

Dongting Biluochun

洞庭碧螺春 dòng tíng bì luó chūn

ALSO KNOWN AS
Green Snail Spring
WHERE IT'S FROM
Dongting, Jiangsu (江蘇 jiāng sū)

Also one of the more famous Chinese tea styles, Biluochun is best known for two things. First is its spiral shape: Biluochun literally means "green snail spring", with "snail" referring to the unique processing step that shapes the tea leaves into tight, snail-resembling coils. Its second distinguishing feature is its sharp fruity aroma, commonly referred to as "shockingly fragrant" (嚇煞人香 xià shā rén xiāng). The Tai Hu (Lake Tai) region from which this tea originates, is known for having apricot and peach trees growing alongside the tea shrubs, which is said to give the tea a fresh and fruity taste.

Anji Baicha

安吉白茶 ān jí bái chá

ALSO KNOWN AS
Anji White Tea
WHERE IT'S FROM
Anji, Zhejiang

Anji Baicha — literally "Anji white tea" in Chinese — is in fact a green tea. Its name is derived from its cultivar, the Baiye 1 ("white leaf 1" 白葉一號 bái yè yī hào) which grows pale white-colored buds during the spring. Anji Baicha is special because of its relatively short harvesting period: the buds only remain pale white for a short amount of time. When late spring or summer comes around, the buds return to a normal green hue. The color of this tea is famously described as "white jade", and its taste profile is first and foremost fresh, with a hint of sweetness and no bitterness at all. Its sweet aftertaste is said to last for up to a couple of hours.

Lushan Yunwu

盧山雲霧 lú shān yún wù

ALSO KNOWN AS
Lushan Cloud Mist Tea
WHERE IT'S FROM
Lushan, Jiangxi (江西 jiāng xī)

Yunwu, which literally means "cloud mist", can be used as a general descriptor for any Gaoshan (High Mountain) teas, but Lushan Yunwu is one of the more famous and prestigious varieties in mainland China. Grown on Lushan Mountain in Jiangxi province, the tea trees are exposed to clouds and a ton of mist for about half the year. The tea is known for its strong fragrance and enduring flavors. Appearance-wise, the finished tea is tightly curled and has a vibrant jade color.

Huangshan Maofeng

黃山毛峰 huáng shān máo fēng

WHERE IT'S FROM
Huangshan, Anhui (安徽 ān huī)

A Gaoshancha (High Mountain Tea) from the famous scenic region of Huangshan in Anhui Province, Huangshan Maofeng is a top-tier green tea that's known for its visible silvery fuzz. Maofeng means "fur peaks", which alludes to its relatively large leaf size and tender, hairy tips. The leaves are very delicately processed — wilted, then kill-greened, rolled and oven-dried — which helps to preserve the silvery fuzz, resulting in an ivory brew with no bitterness and a lingering sweet taste. The tea leaves also famously "dance", floating straight up in the water before sinking to the bottom.

Taiping Houkui

太平猴魁 tài píng hóu kuí

ALSO KNOWN AS
Monkey King Tea, Monkey Tea
WHERE IT'S FROM
Huangshan City, Anhui

Hailing from Houkeng (猴坑 hóu kēng) in Huangshan City, Anhui, this tea presents arguably the most aesthetically pleasing final product. The long, flattened tea leaves are a stunning vibrant green hue, and clearly showcase the bud and its two leaves. The leaves are often marked with a unique basket pattern due to a specific pressing step in the drying stage. Use a glass cup or pot when brewing this tea, and you'll get to see the flat leaves slowly "blooming". The tea is known for its floral and refreshing flavors and has a brisk sweetness that lingers at the back of one's throat.

Xinyang Maojian

信陽毛尖 xìn yáng máo jiān

WHERE IT'S FROM
Xinyang, Henan (河南 hé nán)

Xinyang Maojian is famously known for its delicate leaves and robust flavors. Maojian — literally "fur tip" — refers not only to its abundant silvery hairs, but also to its signature thin pine-needle-like dried leaves. Consisting of one bud and one leaf, Xinyang Maojian is from the Dabieshan mountain region (大別山 dà bié shān), where it's colder and covered in snow during winter — the result is smaller, tender leaves. The tea is fresh yet bold, often described as having a soft savoriness, with meaty notes.

The plucking time is especially important in determining tea quality. Top-tier Xinyang Maojian teas are made from leaves plucked before the end of spring, and are classified as Snow Bud (雪芽 xuě yá) teas. Lesser-grade teas use leaves plucked after summer and are called Jade Bud (翠芽 cuì yá) and Jade Green (翠綠 cuì lǜ). Note that these classifications can also be applied to other green tea styles, although they are more commonly used for Xinyang Maojian.

Lu'an Guapian

六安瓜片 lù ān guā piàn

WHERE IT'S FROM
Lu'an, Anhui

Lu'an Guapian is an odd one out among green teas. The plucking standard is unusual, calling for larger leaves only, without any buds or stems, resulting in a distinctive plump shape that gives the tea its name of Guapian or "melon seed". Guapian tea is made strictly from the second piece of tea leaf, counting from the top. It tastes nothing like your usual green tea, with less of the grassiness, and more of a thick, sweet, almost smoky character. That's because the leaves go through three separate drying stages in the oven after wilting and kill-green. Unlike other green teas, Lu'an Guapian can be aged, just like Sheng Pu'er. Aged Lu'an (老六安 lǎo lù ān) provides an amber brew and an earthy taste profile.

Harvest Periods

MINGQIAN

明前 míng qián

Mingqian means before Qingming (清明 qīng míng). This term is used to denote a spring tea made from leaves plucked before Qingming Festival, which falls on the first week of March on the lunar calendar and early April on the Gregorian calendar. This is important because the first spring plucks are considered more tender and flavorful, full of the nutrients stored throughout winter.

YUHOU

雨後 yǔ hòu

Yuhou, meaning "after rain", refers to tea made from leaves plucked after Guyu ("grain rain" 穀雨 gǔ yǔ), the sixth of 24 solar terms (節氣 jié qì). The solar terms are a traditional system created by farmers to single out 24 days throughout the year. Each of the days marks important changes in weather and season, such as the summer and winter solstice, based on the position of the sun. Guyu is the solar term that indicates an increase in rainfall, marking the end of spring and the coming of summer. Green tea made from leaves picked after spring is generally considered lower grade.

WHITE TEA

白茶 bái chá

Shoumei

壽眉 shòu méi

ALSO KNOWN AS
Gongmei (貢眉 gòng méi)
WHERE IT'S FROM
Fuding, Fujian (福建 fú jiàn)

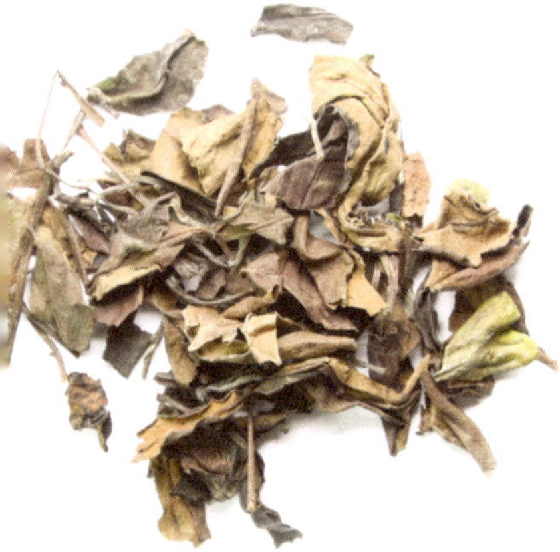

If you've been to a dim sum restaurant, you've heard of Shoumei, literally meaning "longevity eyebrows". It is the most well known and most produced white tea style, made with big, broken leaves and very little buds. The liquor is a deep yellow, and the signature taste profile is a honey aroma with fruity notes. Shoumei can be aged and sometimes appears in the form of a compressed tea cake. The cake form is a matter of practicality, since loose leaves are harder to carry around. Furthermore, just like with Pu'er, the tea cake shape is said to allow the leaves to age slowly and evenly. Gongmei is often considered a premium grade of shoumei.

Baimudan

白牡丹 bái mǔ dān

ALSO KNOWN AS
White Peony
WHERE IT'S FROM
Fuding, Fujian

Baimudan — meaning "white peony" — hints at the way the tea "blooms" when brewed. This tea is made from the same cultivar and uses the same processing steps as Baihao Yinzhen; the difference lies in its plucking standard. Baihao Yinzhen is made with only buds, while Baimudan comprises of a bud and one to two leaves. As with Baihao Yinzhen, good Baimudan features dry leaves covered in white hairs. This tea produces an apricot liquor, an elegant aroma, and a mellow taste with a brush of fruitiness.

Fujian White Tea

While Fuding (福鼎 fú dǐng) is the most prestigious city in Fujian for white tea production, nearby Zhenghe (政和 zhèng hé) and Fu'an (福安 fú ān) are also known for their white tea products.

Baihao Yinzhen

白毫銀針 bái háo yín zhēn

ALSO KNOWN AS
White Hair Silver Needle
WHERE IT'S FROM
Fuding, Fujian

This tea is usually regarded as the most premium among white teas. Baihao means "white hair" and refers to the tea's defining characteristic: the lavish layer of silvery white hairs on the plump and tender tea buds (no tea leaves are used). Yinzhen means "silver needles" and alludes to the tapering of the buds to a sharp, needle-like point. The minimal processing preserves the abundant white hairs and creates a silky brew with a soft and clean floral aroma. While Shoumei and Baimudan are often aged, Baihao Yinzhen is best consumed fresh within the year that it was produced.

Yueguangbai

月光白 yuè guāng bái

ALSO KNOWN AS
Moonlight White
WHERE IT'S FROM
Yunnan province (雲南 yún nán)

Yueguangbai, meaning "moonlight white", is a label used for all white teas that come from Yunnan. The tea is made using buds and leaves strictly from the native large-leaf assamica tea plant. The reason for its name is due to the unique process of withering the tea leaves in the shade (instead of the conventional sun). The prolonged withering results in a stronger and richer tea. The deeper liquor smells like wood and honey and gives a layered sweetness.

YELLOW TEA

黄茶 huáng chá

Junshan Yinzhen

君山銀針 jūn shān yín zhēn

ALSO KNOWN AS
Junshan Silver Needle
WHERE IT'S FROM
Yueyang, Hunan (湖南 hú nán)

The most widely known yellow tea, Junshan Yinzhen is produced in limited quantities and includes only tender buds. Junzhan Yinzhen is famously nicknamed "gold-rimmed jade" (金鑲玉 jīn xiāng yù), depicting beautiful yellowed buds coated in white hair.

Huoshan Huangya

霍山黃芽 huò shān huáng yá

WHERE IT'S FROM
Huoshan, Anhui

Huoshan Huangya is one of the easiest yellow teas to find on the market. Huoshan refers to Huoshan county in Anhui, while Huangya or "yellow buds" is a name that's shared among three types of yellow teas — the others being the rarer Mengding Huangya (蒙頂黃芽 méng dǐng huáng yá) from Sichuan and Mogan Huangya (莫干黃芽 mò gàn huáng yá) from Zhejiang. It consists of one bud and one leaf, and its making is extremely laborious. It has a distinct chestnut flavor, combined with the fresh and floral fragrance that is typical in green teas.

WULONG TEA

烏龍 wū lóng

MAINLAND CHINA

Anxi Tieguanyin

安溪鐵觀音 ān xī tiě guān yīn

ALSO KNOWN AS
Iron Goddess

WHERE IT'S FROM
Anxi, Fujian

Tieguanyin is defined by its ball shape, floral fragrance, and powerful aftertaste. Tieguanyin from Anxi usually consists of loosely curled semi-balls that are moderately roast-dried, with floral and fruity notes. Lovers of Tieguanyin, which means "iron goddess of mercy", often look for the telltale Yinyun ("goddess rhyme" 音韻 yīn yùn) in their tea, which refers to the tangy sensation one gets at the back of the throat after drinking it. Lightly roasted (清香 qīng xiāng) Tieguanyin has also become popular with younger drinkers in recent years.

A popular phrase that's used to describe Tieguanyin is Spring Water, Autumn Aroma (春水秋香 chūn shuǐ qiū xiāng), which means that its spring tea is great in taste and mouthfeel, while its autumn tea is more aromatic. Because of Tieguanyin's popularity, tea makers have been increasingly experimenting with similar tea styles using different cultivars. Notable ones include the Anxi Huangjingui (安溪黃金桂 ān xī huáng jīn guì), Anxi Benshan (安溪本山 ān xī běn shān), Anxi Maoxie (安溪毛蟹 ān xī máo xiè), and Anxi Jinguanyin (安溪金觀音 ān xī jīn guān yīn). They can all be classified as southern Fujian wulong (閩南烏龍 mǐn nán wū lóng).

Wuyi Yancha

武夷岩茶 wǔ yí yán chá

ALSO KNOWN AS
Wuyi Rock Tea
WHERE IT'S FROM
Wuyi, Fujian

Wuyi Yancha (aka Wuyi Rock Tea) is a subcategory of wulong tea, and refers to all teas grown in the very rocky terrain known as the Danxia Landform in the Wuyi region. It is the most famous of the Northern Fujian wulong (閩北烏龍 mǐn běi wū lóng). When it comes to Wuyi Yancha, it's better to first let go of any assumptions you have about wulong. Unlike most wulong teas that boast a strong floral or fruity fragrance, Wuyi Yancha is all about the heavy roast and signature dark, bold flavor known as Yanyun ("rock rhyme" 岩韻 yán yùn). What gives the tea this distinctive mouthfeel is the rocky terrain on which it's grown. The tea leaves are tightly curled into plump and evenly shaped dark strips.

The general classification for Wuyi Yancha is:

ZHENGYAN

("center yancha" 正岩 zhèng yán)
Teas grown inside the Wuyi protected area. The most highly revered locations are the Three Pits Two Creeks (三坑兩澗 sān kēng liǎng jiàn), which include Niulankeng (牛欄坑 niú lán kēng), Huiyuankeng (慧園坑 huì yuán kēng), Daoshuikeng (倒水坑 dào shuǐ kēng), Liuxiangjian (流香澗 liú xiāng jiàn), and Wuyuanjian (悟源澗 wù yuán jiàn).

BANYAN

("half yancha" 半岩 bàn yán)
Teas grown in the immediate area surrounding the Wuyi protected area. Banyan teas are more affordable and fragrant, but have less Yanyun. Well-known locations include Xingcun (星村 xīng cūn) and Xiaowuyi (小武夷 xiǎo wǔ yí).

ZHOUCHA

("provincial tea" 洲茶 zhōu chá)
Teas grown in the plantations far outside the protected area in the region. The majority of yancha sold in the market is zhoucha.

FOUR FAMOUS WUYI YANCHAS

四大名欉 sì dà míng cóng

Wuyi Tieluohan

武夷鐵羅漢 wǔ yí tiě luó hàn

This tea, as its name suggests, is made from the Tieluohan cultivar. Tieluohan literally means "iron monk", and this tea is suitably known for its tough and blunt flavor profile.

Wuyi Shuijingui

武夷水金龜 wǔ yí shuǐ jīn guī

This tea is made from the Shuijingui ("water golden turtle") cultivar and consists of rounder and thinner leaves. This is one of the more challenging varietals to turn into tea. First-rate Shuijingui is subtly fruity and full-bodied.

Wuyi Baijiguan

武夷白雞冠 wǔ yí bái jī guàn

Baijiguan means "white cockscomb", since the cultivar's leaves are pale yellowish and open like a cockscomb. The finished tea also features significantly lighter-colored dry leaves compared to other Wuyi Yanchas.

Wuyi Dahongpao

武夷大紅袍 wǔ yí dà hóng páo

ALSO KNOWN AS

Big Red Robe

Dahongpao has long been a celebrity tea. It was the tea Mao Zedong gifted President Nixon in 1972. Former Chinese president Jiang Zemin also gave Hong Kong's first Chief Executive this tea to mark the 1997 handover. Dahongpao originally referred to the six mother trees on Jiulongke (九龍窠 jiǔ lóng kē) in the Tianxinyan (天心岩 tiān xīn yán) area on Wuyi Mountain — but these trees are no longer harvested. Dahongpao today mostly refers to teas made from the Beidou 1 cultivar (北斗一號 běi dǒu yī hào), which is propagated from the mother trees or a blend of cultivars to best showcase the complex and pleasing experience of Yanyun.

OTHER WUYI YANCHA CULTIVARS

WUYI ROUGUI

武夷肉桂 wǔ yí ròu guì

This tea is loved for its distinct notes of cassia cinnamon. The more sought-after varietals are Niulankeng Rougui (牛欄坑肉桂 niú lán kēng ròu guì) and Matouyan Rougui (馬頭岩肉桂 mǎ tóu yán ròu guì).

WUYI SHUIXIAN

武夷水仙 wǔ yí shuǐ xiān

This tea has the largest and thickest leaves of all Wuyi Yanchas. An especially sought-after sub-style is the Laocong Shuixian (老欉水仙 lǎo cóng shuǐ xiān) made from Shuixian cultivars that are 50 years or older.

Fenghuang Dancong

鳳凰單欉 fèng huáng dān cóng

ALSO KNOWN AS
Phoenix Dancong, Phoenix Single Bush
WHERE IT'S FROM
Phoenix Mountain, Guangdong (廣東 guǎng dōng)

Fenghuang Dancong is a very showy tea, known for being almost over-the-top aromatic and fondly described as "drinkable perfume". Fenghuang refers to the Phoenix Mountain (鳳凰山 fèng huáng shān) area in Guangdong province where this tea is from, and Dancong, literally "single bush", refers to tea consisting of leaves from a single cultivar or a single plant. Wudong (烏崠 wū dōng) is the highest and most sought-after peak in Phoenix Mountain. Visually, this tea has long and slightly curled strip-shaped dark leaves. Commercially, this tea is classified by 10 signature fragrances, but as the cultivar is generally perceived as more important in determining tea quality, it is also useful to differentiate by cultivars.

TEN SIGNATURE FRAGRANCES

1. **Gardenia Fragrance** (黃梔香 huáng zhī xiāng)
2. **Orchid Fragrance** (芝蘭香 zhī lán xiāng)
3. **Honey Orchid Fragrance** (蜜蘭香 mì lán xiāng)
4. **Osthmanthus Fragrance** (桂花香 guì huā xiāng)
5. **Magnolia Fragrance** (玉蘭香 yù lán xiāng)
6. **Almond Fragrance** (杏仁香 xìng rén xiāng)
7. **Tuberose Fragrance** (夜來香 yè lái xiāng)
8. **Ginger Flower Fragrance** (薑花香 jiāng huā xiāng)
9. **Jasmine Fragrance** (茉莉香 mò lì xiāng)
10. **Cassia Cinnamon Fragrance** (肉桂香 ròu guì xiāng)

EIGHT CULTIVARS

1. **Baxian** (八仙 bā xiān): obvious citrusy notes
2. **Songzhong** (宋種 sòng zhǒng): strong with notes of herbs and maple
3. **Zhilan Xiang / Orchid Fragrance** (芝蘭香 zhī lán xiāng): sweet, floral, and elegant
4. **Baiye** (白葉 bái yè): most common cultivar; strong notes of peach and honey
5. **Wuye** (烏葉 wū yè): also a common cultivar; grassy and floral with a subtle nuttiness
6. **Yashi Xiang** ("duck poo fragrance" 鴨屎香 yā shǐ xiāng): buttery with floral and tangerine flavors
7. **Juduozai** (鋸朵仔 jù duǒ zǎi): small leaves; visible white hairs; often marketed as Almond Fragrance; thick and nutty
8. **Milan Xiang / Honey Orchid Fragrance** (蜜蘭香 mì lán xiāng): thick and creamy

TAIWAN

Wenshan Baozhong

文山包種 wén shān bāo zhǒng

WHERE IT'S FROM

Pinglin, Taipei (台北 tái běi)

Clean and pristine: that's what you get with Wenshan Baozhong. This strip-shaped tea from Pinglin is one of the most representative of Taiwanese wulong teas. With the lowest oxidation levels (under 20 percent) out of all wulong teas, Baozhong makes a very pale green brew and is grassy and wonderfully creamy, with notes of almond. It's made from leaves of the Qingxin (青心 qīng xīn) cultivar. The name Baozhong, meaning "wrapped type", comes from the traditional way this tea was wrapped in paper and sold. Baozhong teas are often graded based on how fragrant they are, and the best ones contain a subtle milky note.

Muzha Tieguanyin

木柵鐵觀音 mù zhà tiě guān yīn

ALSO KNOWN AS

Iron Goddess

WHERE IT'S FROM

Muzha, Taipei

Tieguanyin from Muzha, Taipei usually has a more tightly rolled ball shape and undergoes a more intricate roast-drying process than the Anxi Tieguanyin found in Fujian. Due to the more complex and drawn-out roasting procedure, this tea gives a dark amber brew with rich notes of orchid, caramel and smoke. Light roasts (清香 qīng xiāng) have also become more popular and widely available.

Gaoshancha

高山茶 gāo shān chá

ALSO KNOWN AS

High Mountain Tea, High Cold Tea (高冷茶 gāo lěng chá)

WHERE IT'S FROM

Various provinces in Taiwan

Gaoshancha (aka High Mountain Tea) refers to any tea that's made from plants grown at an elevation higher than 1,000 meters. Gaoshan wulong teas are usually curled into tightly shaped glossy balls. The cultivar — typically Qingxin, Jinxuan (金萱 jīn xuān), Cuiyu (翠玉 cuì yù), and Sijichun (四季春 sì jì chūn) — from which the tea is made, is not as important a factor as the tea's distinctive terroir and climate. The high elevation, low temperatures, high moisture levels and minimum sunlight result in thick leaves and an incredibly deep and nuanced flavor profile, which is referred to by many as Shantouqi ("mountain essence" 山頭氣 shān tóu qì). It often translates to a strong but elegant floral aroma, pleasant bittersweetness in the back of one's throat, and an enduring aftertaste. The most well-known Gaoshan regions are:

1. **Alishan** (阿里山 ā lǐ shān): most famous of all Gaoshancha teas; thick and mellow; complex, aromatic, with notes of sugarcane and orchid

2. **Lishan** (梨山 lí shān): strong but refined; sweet and pleasantly astringent

3. **Dayuling** (大禹嶺 dà yǔ lǐng): the highest Gaoshancha region at 2,400 meters; thick body with a deep richness often accompanied by notes of fruits or chocolate

4. **Shanlinxi** (杉林溪 shān lín xī): distinctive citrusy aroma, refreshing woody notes, and a refined sweetness; compared to Alishan, it tastes more airy and has a weaker aftertaste

Oriental Beauty

東方美人 dōng fāng měi rén

ALSO KNOWN AS

Dongfang Meiren, Baihao Wulong (白毫烏龍 bái háo wū lóng), Pong Feng Tea (椪風茶 pèng fēng chá), Braggart's Tea

WHERE IT'S FROM

Hsinchu city (新竹 xīn zhú)

Oriental Beauty is the most heavily oxidized wulong tea (70 to 80 percent oxidation), resulting in a dark red liquor that looks more like red tea. Its most distinctive characteristic is its use of only leaves that have been bitten by a special tiny leafhopper called the Jacobiasca formosana (小綠葉蟬 xiǎo lǜ yè chán), which causes the plant to release more aromatic compounds. It's made from the Qingxin Damao (青心大冇 qīng xīn dà mǎo) cultivar and is the only wulong that includes buds as well as leaves. When purchasing, look for a visible layer of white down on the leaves, which is indicative of quality and careful processing. The processing is very laborious, as the make-green stage needs to be carefully and manually managed. The tea has rich and delightful honey notes, resembling a refreshing sweet nectar.

Dongding Wulong

凍頂烏龍 dòng dǐng wū lóng

WHERE IT'S FROM

Nantou county (南投 nán tóu)

Another very famous Taiwanese wulong, this is a ball-shaped tea made from the Qingxin cultivar in the Dongding Mountain area in Nantou, defined by a skillfully managed make-green process and more mellow and delicate flavors. The make-green stage is repeated multiple times until the tea master is satisfied with the oxidation levels. The leaves are then kill-greened, rolled, and dried. The full-bodied brew is known for its complex transition from smoky-flavored to floral and fruity, after multiple steeps.

Jinxuan Wulong

金萱烏龍 jīn xuān wū lóng

WHERE IT'S FROM

Various regions in Taiwan

Jinxuan refers to a cultivar unique to Taiwan, developed by the government-backed Tea Research and Extension Station. It's very widely available and is beloved by many for its buttery mouthfeel and obvious Naixiang (奶香 nǎi xiāng), or fragrant milky flavor. Jinxuan tea has light floral and citrusy notes, and its leaves can also be processed into red teas.

Sijichun

四季春 sì jì chūn

ALSO KNOWN AS

Four Seasons Spring

WHERE IT'S FROM

Various regions in Taiwan

Similar to Jinxuan, Sijichun refers to a cultivar that's specific to Taiwan. The plant grows and is ready to harvest all year round, making it a widely available tea style. Good Sijichun teas are light and bright, with vegetal and floral undertones. It's also a very commonly found tea base in modern Chinese tea drink brands.

RED TEA

紅茶 hóng chá

MAINLAND CHINA

Qimen Hongcha

祁門紅茶 qí mén hóng chá

ALSO KNOWN AS
Qimen Red Tea, Keemun Black Tea
WHERE IT'S FROM
Qimen, Anhui

Qimen Hongcha is arguably China's most highly regarded red tea, known for its super strong fragrance and deep, mellow sweetness spanning a wide range of delightful flavors from chocolate to ripe fruit. Qimen is a county in the city of Huangshan, and red teas from the region are often all called Qimen Hongcha. This tea comes in both small and evenly shaped broken pieces of leaves and buds called Hao Ya (毫芽 háo yá) — meaning "tiny buds", as well as tightly twisted strip-shaped whole leaves called Maofeng (毛峰 máo fēng) — meaning "fur tips". Whole-leaf Qimen is often more coveted, as it demands greater labor and tastes more complex and mellow. Whichever style you're after, remember to look for dark but glossy dry leaves, an obvious sweet aroma — and the more golden tips, the better.

Lapsang Souchong

正山小種 zhèng shān xiǎo zhǒng

ALSO KNOWN AS
Zhengshan Xiaozhong
WHERE IT'S FROM
Wuyi Mountain, Fujian

Lapsang Souchong (literally "authentic mountain small variety" in Chinese) is made in the restricted reserve area of Tongmuguan (桐木關 tóng mù guān) in the Wuyi Mountain region, which is widely regarded as the birthplace of red tea. The defining feature of this tea is a unique smoking technique. Authentic Lapsang Souchong has to be made in a three- to four-story Qinglou (清樓 qīng lóu) hut — which, fun fact, sounds identical to "brothel house" in Chinese — where a large pinewood-burning fireplace sits at the bottom level, imparting a unique smoky scent onto the leaves. Besides its distinctive smokiness, this tea is known for notes of longan and roasted chestnuts. Similarly smoked red tea from areas other than Tongmuguan are often referred to as Yanxiaozhong (煙小種 yān xiǎo zhǒng).

Jinjunmei

金駿眉 jīn jùn méi

ALSO KNOWN AS
Golden Fine Brows
WHERE IT'S FROM
Wuyi Mountain, Fujian

Despite red tea's popularity abroad, it has long been considered a lower-grade tea by Chinese tea drinkers for its perceived inferiority to green tea and for being primarily an export tea. Jinjunmei is one of the first red tea styles to be enthusiastically embraced by Chinese tea drinkers. It was introduced to the market in the 2000s and became an instant hit. It's a premium tea from Tongmuguan and made from only young buds. It is beloved for the thickness of its tea soup and its fragrance. Other varieties include "silver fine brows" (銀駿眉 yín jùn méi), made from one bud and one leaf.

The gongfu method of brewing in action

Gongfu: A style and a method

When it comes to red tea, the term Gongfu (工夫 **gōng fū**) actually refers to a specific style of red tea and is written differently in Chinese from the Gongfu (功夫 **gōng fū**) method of tea brewing. Confusingly, Gongfucha (工夫茶 **gōng fū chá**) is also a generic label applied to any teas that are handmade.

Academically speaking, red tea is classified into three general styles. Gongfu Hongcha (工夫紅茶 **gōng fū hóng chá**) refers to whole-leaf red tea that is hand-crafted and tightly twisted into strips. Xiaozhong Hongcha (小種紅茶 **xiǎo zhǒng hóng chá**) refers to tea made from the unique Qinglou smoking technique (see Lapsong Souchong). Hongsuicha (紅碎茶 **hóng suì chá**) is red tea made from broken leaves and buds — it's the equivalent of western-style CTC (cut-tear-curl) commodity tea.

The Gongfu method of brewing, on the other hand, refers to a flash brewing technique that uses a large amount of tea leaves and very little water. With this style, water is poured into the teapot and then drained out immediately. The method is popular for brewing wulong teas like Fenghuang Dancong and Wuyi Yancha.

Dianhong

滇紅 diān hóng

WHERE IT'S FROM
Yunnan province

Dianhong refers to all red teas from Yunnan province that are made from the Fengqing Dayezhong (鳳慶大葉種 fèng qìng dà yè zhǒng) cultivar of the native large-leaf assamica variety. It is a relatively new tea style but has quickly become very popular. Compared to small-leaf red teas, Dianhong is known for its more substantial body. The liquor is a bright golden orange, tasting distinctively of black sugar and lychee. A popular sub-style is the bud-only Dianhong Jinya or "golden bud" (滇紅金芽 diān hóng jīn yá), also called Jinzhen "golden needle" (金針 jīn zhēn) or Jinsi "golden thread" (金絲 jīn sī).

Bailin Gongfu

白琳工夫 bái lín gōng fū

WHERE IT'S FROM
Fuding, Fujian

Part of the Minhong Gongfu (閩紅工夫 mǐn hóng gōng fū) Fujian red tea trio, Bailin Gongfu from the city of Fuding is the most famous of the lot. The tightly twisted strips are accented with golden, hairy tips. A more affordable red tea style, it is full-bodied and malty, with notes of honey and sweet potato. The liquor is a beautiful bright clay red. The other two Minhong Gongfu teas are Tanyang Gongfu (坦洋工夫 tǎn yáng gōng fū) from the city of Fuan and Zhenghe Gongfu (政和工夫 zhèng hé gōng fū) from Zhenghe county.

Sun Moon Lake Red Tea

日月潭紅茶 rì yuè tán hóng chá

ALSO KNOWN AS

Riyuetan Hongcha, Shuishalian Hongcha (水沙連紅茶 shuǐ shā lián hóng chá)

WHERE IT'S FROM

Nantou county

Taiwan's most famous red tea, Sun Moon Lake Red Tea is grown in the Sun Moon Lake area in Yuchi township, Nantou. It is made from the large-leaf assamica, which was planted in the area in 1925 during the Japanese occupation. It is more subdued and has a light floral fragrance.

The most highly regarded tea cultivars in the region include No. 7 Taiwan (台茶7號 tái chá qī hào), No. 8 Taiwan (台茶8號 tái chá bā hào), No. 18 Taiwan (台茶18號 tái chá shí bā hào), Assam (阿薩姆 ā sà mǔ), and Pengshu Hongcha (膨鼠紅茶 péng shǔ hóng chá). No. 18 Taiwan, in particular, has won many awards and is a hybrid between the Taiwanese tea tree and the Assam tea tree from Myanmar. It is beloved for its incredibly smooth and rich mouthfeel, and its slight notes of cinnamon and mint.

Jinxuan Hongcha

金萱紅茶 jīn xuān hóng chá

WHERE IT'S FROM

Various regions in Taiwan

Jinxuan is a cultivar that's unique to Taiwan. While it is more often turned into a wulong tea, it is increasingly being processed as a red tea as well.

BLACK TEA

黑茶 hēi chá

Pu'er

普洱 pǔ ěr

WHERE IT'S FROM
Yunnan province

Pu'er is one of the most difficult Chinese teas to appreciate, with many calling it an acquired taste. Pu'er city was historically the tea-trading hub of Yunnan. For a tea to be authentically Pu'er, it must be grown in Yunnan, made from the native large-leaf assamica Dayezhong (大葉種 dà yè zhǒng) cultivar, and sun-dried. Pu'er made from trees over 100 years old (or planted during the Ming and Qing Dynasties) are referred to as Gushucha ("ancient tree tea" 古樹茶 gǔ shù chá) and are considered more premium and nutritious. There are two distinct types of Pu'er: Sheng Pu'er (生普 shēng pǔ) and Shu Pu'er (熟普 shú pǔ). Both types start out as a minimally oxidized green tea-like raw product known as Maocha (毛茶 máo chá).

SHENG PU'ER

生普 shēng pǔ

Sheng Pu'er, meaning "raw Pu'er", is the most commonly enjoyed style of Pu'er in China, and can be academically classified as a sun-dried green tea. The plucking standard is one bud and one to three leaves. The leaves are left to wilt for a few hours, kill-greened, rolled, and then dried. They are then typically steamed and pressed into a solid, round cake form for retail sale.

Sheng Pu'er is meant to be aged over time — preferably kept in a dry, non-airtight, odor-free environment to promote both oxidation and fermentation. Well-aged tea cakes fetch an outrageous price on the market. While aged Sheng Pu'er is highly sought after, many also enjoy the tea un-aged or fresh.

SHU PU'ER

熟普 shú pǔ

Yunnan's Pu'er tea became popular in the city of Hong Kong in the 1960s. But the great distance between the two destinations meant that the teas tended to develop a deeper color and richer flavors by the time they reached Hong Kong. Mainland Chinese tea makers sought to reproduce this particular Hong Kong-style of Pu'er for its export markets and in 1973, Yunnan's Kunming Tea Factory adapted the wet-piling technique (traditionally used to make black tea) to its Pu'er Maocha and successfully produced the first Shu Pu'er, which literally means "ripe Pu'er" in Chinese.

Shu Pu'er is known for its mellow tones and earthy aromas. The tea soup is commonly described as Zhuganhong ("pork liver red" 豬肝紅 zhū gān hóng). While Shu Pu'er can be stored for up to 10 years, it doesn't age as gracefully compared to the Sheng Pu'er.

What's in a Name?

During the late 1990s, Pu'er caught the attention of the Chinese tea world, with many looking to invest in and collect Pu'er tea cakes. By 2007, the year the Pu'er bubble burst, prices for the tea had increased more than tenfold.

A Pu'er tea's value is most closely tied to its location of origin. The name of the mountain or village from which the Pu'er is grown is often labeled on the product, and each region comes with its own distinct flavor profile. There are three main regions: Xishuangbanna (西雙版納 xī shuāng bǎn nà) — often referred to as Jinghong (景洪 jǐng hóng) — is the most historic and usually the most expensive. Some of the most well-known Banna regions include Nannuoshan (南糯山 nán nuò shān), Nakka (那卡 nà kǎ), Jingmai (景邁 jǐng mài), and Bulangshan (布朗山 bù lǎng shān), which is home to Laobanzhang (老班章 lǎo bān zhāng), where the most expensive Pu'er products in the market are produced. There are no label standardizations or regulations in the market, so buyer beware!

Lincang (臨滄 lín cāng) is the second of the three main regions and is west of Xishuangbanna. Its most famous village is Bingdao (冰島 bīng dǎo), literally "ice island", and its Pu'er tea is currently one of the most expensive on the market.

The last of the three regions is Jingdong (景東 jǐng dōng), which is the most affordable of the three. There are so many mountains and villages in Yunnan and around Pu'er, and each boasts its own unique traits.

Pu'er teas are sold in various shapes, most commonly nowadays in loose-leaf (散茶 sǎn chá) or round tea cake (餅茶 bǐng chá) forms. They can also be compressed into squares (方茶 fāng chá), rectangular bricks (磚茶 zhuān chá), bird-nest shapes (沱茶 tuó chá), melon shapes (金瓜茶 jīn guā chá), mushroom shapes (緊茶 jǐn chá), or into dried mandarins (陳皮普洱 chén pí pǔ ěr) and bamboos (竹筒茶 zhú tǒng chá).

Anhua Fuzhuan

安化茯砖 ān huà fú zhuān

ALSO KNOWN AS
Anhua Brick Tea, Golden Flower Brick Tea
WHERE IT'S FROM
Anhua, Hunan

Anhua Heicha (安化黑茶 ān huà hēi chá), also known as Anhua Black Tea, is one of the most widely available black teas in mainland China. Anhua Heicha can be sold loose-leaf, or in brick form like the Anhua Fuzhuan (aka Anhua Brick Tea). The tea leaves are first kill-greened, then rolled, wet-piled and dried. More premium leaves are made into loose-leaf tea, while the rest are often steamed and compressed into bricks. To make Anhua Fuzhuan, tea leaves are inoculated with Jinhua ("golden flower" 金花 jīn huā), a type of mold spore, before being placed in a warm chamber for up to 20 days to encourage the growth of mold. The tea yields a deep amber liquor and tastes smooth and mellow.

Lu'an Heicha

六安黑茶 lù ān hēi chá

ALSO KNOWN AS
Lu'an Tea, Lu'an Dark Tea, Lu'an Basket Tea
WHERE IT'S FROM
Lu'an, Anhui

Lu'an Heicha is known for its distinctive basket packaging and a tangy fragrance. The pluck standard is usually one bud and two to three leaves The leaves are kill-greened, then rolled, wet-piled and dried. They are then sorted by quality, steamed, packed into bamboo baskets lined with bamboo leaves, and dried again. Lu'an Heicha is said to possess a delicate bamboo aroma. Most Lu'an Heichas are sold after two to three years of storage.

CHINA'S 10 MOST FAMOUS TEAS

(an ever-changing list)

There are actually many purported Top 10 lists of China's most famous teas out there, published by government departments, official newspapers or tea expos. The below list shows the 10 most frequently included in such lists.

green tea
XIHU LONGJING
西湖龍井 xī hú lóng jǐng

green tea
DONGTING BILUOCHUN
洞庭碧螺春 dòng tíng bì luó chūn

wulong
ANXI TIEGUANYIN
安溪鐵觀音 ān xī tiě guān yīn

FLORAL TEA

花茶 huā chá

Jasmine Tea

茉莉香片 mò lì xiāng piàn

WHERE IT'S FROM

Fuzhou, Fujian

Jasmine tea is the best known among floral teas. Plucked jasmine flowers are laid out on a flat surface at 1 to 2 degrees Celsius above room temperature to allow them to bloom and release their fragrance. The flowers are then usually mixed together with green tea leaves and placed in a warm and moist environment overnight.

When the mixture reaches the desired results, it is oven-dried and then cooled. Jasmine tea now comes in many different forms, from loose leaf to sphere-shaped. A famous sphere-shaped variation is the Dragon Pearl Jasmine Tea (龍團珠茉莉花茶 lóng tuán zhū mò lì huā chá). Jasmine tea makes a vibrant yellow brew, is highly fragrant, and tastes bright and crisp.

green tea
HUANGSHAN MAOFENG
黄山毛峰 huáng shān máo fēng

yellow tea
JUNSHAN YINZHEN
君山銀針 jūn shān yín zhēn

red tea
QIMEN HONGCHA
祁門紅茶 qí mén hóng chá

wulong
WUYI DAHONGPAO
武夷大紅袍 wǔ yí dà hóng páo

green tea
LU'AN GUAPIAN
六安瓜片 lù ān guā piàn

white tea
BAIHAO YINZHEN
白毫銀針 bái háo yín zhēn

black tea
YUNNAN PU'ER
雲南普洱 yún nán pú ěr

A tea plantation in Anxi, Fujian
Photo: Fook Ming Tong

FAMOUS TEA REGIONS

The style or type of tea that's produced in a specific region is contingent on its surrounding climate and environment. Oftentimes, an area naturally begins to specialize in the production of a specific type or style of tea because of its geographical characteristics. We've grouped these distinct tea regions into broad categories for easy visualization.

MAINLAND CHINA

There are more than 20 provinces and over 1,000 counties that produce tea in mainland China. Roughly speaking, China can be divided into four major tea regions.

Xinan Tea Region

西南茶區 xī nán chá qū

Xinan Tea Region (aka High Mountain Tea Region 高原茶區 gāo yuán chá qū), refers to the southwestern part of China and is the most historical tea region in the country. It is believed that this region is where the tea tree originated. It is home to some of the oldest wild tea trees dating back hundreds and even thousands of years. The area includes parts of Yunnan, Guizhou, Sichuan, Tibet, and Chongqing, and is known for its subtropical monsoon climate of generally warm winters and cool summers.

FAMOUS TEAS FROM XINAN

WHERE	TEA TYPE	TEA
SICHUAN	GREEN	**Zhuyeqing** (aka Bamboo Leaf Green 竹葉青 zhú yè qīng) **Yongchuan Xiuya** (永川秀芽 yǒng chuān xiù yá) **Wenjun Nenlu** (文君嫩綠 wén jūn nèn lǜ) **Mengding Ganlu** (蒙頂甘露 mēng dǐng gān lù)
	YELLOW	**Mengding Huangya** (蒙頂黃芽 mēng dǐng huáng yá) (see chapter 4)
	RED	**Zaobaijian** (早白尖 zǎo bái jiān)
	BLACK	**Sichuan Biancha** (四川邊茶 sì chuān biān chá)
YUNNAN	GREEN	**Baohung Tea** (寶洪茶 bǎo hóng chá)
	RED	**Dianhong** (滇紅 diān hóng) (see chapter 4)
GUIZHOU	GREEN	**Duyun Maojian** (都匀毛尖 dū yún máo jiān)

Huanan Tea Region

華南茶區 huá nán chá qū

Huanan refers to southern China and spans Guangdong, Guangxi, Fujian, Hainan and southern Yunnan provinces. The warm and wet climate there is the most suitable out of the four tea regions for tea growing, with favorable conditions for at least 10 months of the year.

FAMOUS TEAS FROM HUANAN

WHERE	TEA TYPE	TEA
YUNNAN	GREEN	**Nannuo Baihao** (南糯白毫 nán nuò bái háo) **Cangshan Xuelu** (蒼山雪綠 cāng shān xuě lǜ) **Yunhai Baihao** (雲海白毫 yún hǎi bái háo)
	WHITE	**Yueguangbai** (aka Moonlight White 月光白 yuè guāng bái) (see chapter 4)
	RED	**Dianhong** (滇紅 diān hóng) (see chapter 4)
	BLACK	**Sheng Pu'er** (生普 shēng pǔ) (see chapter 4) **Shu Pu'er** (熟普 shú pǔ) (see chapter 4)

WHERE	TEA TYPE	TEA
GUANGXI	GREEN	**Guilin Maojian** (桂林毛尖 guì lín máo jiān) **Tantang Maojian** (覃塘毛尖 tán táng máo jiān) **Lingyun Baihao** (凌雲白毫 líng yún bái háo)
	BLACK	**Liubao Sancha** (六堡散茶 liù bǎo sàn chá)
	FLORAL	**Osmanthus Green Tea** (桂花茶 guì huā chá)
GUANGDONG	GREEN	**Gulaocha** (古勞茶 gǔ láo chá)
	WULONG	**Fenghuang Dancong** (aka Phoenix Single Bush 鳳凰單欉 fèng huáng dān cóng) (see chapter 4) **Fenghuang Shuixian** (鳳凰水仙 fèng huáng shuǐ xiān)
	RED	**Yingde Hongcha** (英德紅茶 yīng dé hóng chá)
	FLORAL	**Jasmine Tea** (茉莉花茶 mò lì huā chá) (see chapter 4)
FUJIAN	GREEN	**Tianshan Honglu** (天山烘綠 tiān shān hōng lǜ) **Qijing Tangcha** (七境堂茶 qī jìng táng chá) **Lotus Heart** (蓮心茶 lián xīn chá)
	WULONG	**Anxi Tieguanyin** (鐵觀音 tiě guān yīn) (see chapter 4) **Minbei Shuixian** (閩北水仙 mǐn běi shuǐ xiān) **Fo Shou** (佛手 fó shǒu) **Huangjingui** (黃金桂 huáng jīn guì)
	FLORAL	**Jasmine Tea** (茉莉花茶 mò lì huā chá)

Jiangnan Tea Region

江南茶區 jiāng nán chá qū

The biggest tea-producing region in mainland China, Jiangnan Tea Region refers to the area south of the Yangzi River (aka Changjiang 長江 cháng jiāng) and encompasses Zhejiang, Hunan, Jiangxi, and parts of Fujian, Anhui, Jiangsu, Hubei, Guangxi and Guangdong provinces. With a clear divide between the four seasons, and many tall mountains such as Anhui's Huangshan and Jiangxi's Lushan, the region is home to many famous Chinese teas.

FAMOUS TEAS FROM JIANGNAN

WHERE	TEA TYPE	TEA
HUNAN	GREEN	**Anhua Songzhen** (安化松針 ān huà sōng zhēn) **Gaoqiao Yinfeng** (高橋銀峰 gāo qiáo yín fēng) **Donghu Yinhao** (東湖銀毫 dōng hú yín háo)
	YELLOW	**Junshan Yinzhen** (君山銀針 jūn shān yín zhēn) (see chapter 4) **Weishan Baimaojian** (溈山白毛尖 wéi shān bái máo jiān) **Beigang Maojian** (北港毛尖 běi gǎng máo jiān)
	RED	**Yuehong Gongfu** (越紅功夫 yuè hóng gōng fū)
	BLACK	**Heimaocha** (黑毛茶 hēi máo chá) **Heizhuancha** (黑磚茶 hēi zhuān chá)

WHERE	TEA TYPE	TEA
HUBEI	GREEN	**Enshi Yulu** (恩施玉露 ēn shī yù lù) **Xiazhou Bifeng** (峽州碧峰 xiá zhōu bì fēng) **Jinshui Cuifeng** (金水翠峰 jīn shuǐ cuì fēng)
	RED	**Yihong Gongfu** (宜紅工夫 yí hóng gōng fū)
	BLACK	**Laoqingcha** (老青茶 lǎo qīng chá) **Qingzhuancha** (青磚茶 qīng zhuān chá)
JIANGXI	GREEN	**Lushan Yunwu** (廬山雲霧 lú shān yún wù) (see chapter 4) **Shangrao Baimei** (上饒白眉 shàng ráo bái méi) **Shuangjinglu** (雙井綠 shuāng jǐng lǜ)
FUJIAN	WHITE	**Shoumei** (壽眉 shòu méi) (see chapter 4) **Baihao Yinzhen** (aka White Hair Silver Needle 白毫銀針 bái háo yín zhēn) (see chapter 4) **Baimudan** (aka White Peony 白牡丹 bái mǔ dān) (see chapter 4)
	WULONG	**Wuyi Yancha** (aka Wuyi Rock Tea 武夷岩茶 wǔ yí yán chá) (see chapter 4) **Wuyi Rou Gui** (武夷肉桂 wǔ yí ròu guì) **Baimaohou** (白毛猴 bái máo hóu) **Longxucha** (龍鬚茶 lóng xū chá)
	RED	**Lapsang Souchong** (正山小種 zhèng shān xiǎo zhǒng) (see chapter 4) **Bailin Gongfu** (白琳工夫 bái lín gōng fū) (see chapter 4) **Jinjunmei** (aka Golden Fine Brows 金駿眉 jīn jùn méi) (see chapter 4) **Tanyang Gongfu** (坦洋工夫 tǎn yáng gōng fū) (see chapter 4) **Zhenghe Gongfu** (政和工夫 zhèng hé gōng fū) (see chapter 4)

MORE FROM JIANGNAN ▶

WHERE	TEA TYPE	TEA
ANHUI	GREEN	**Huangshan Maofeng** (黃山毛峰 huáng shān máo fēng) (see chapter 4) **Taiping Houkui** (太平猴魁 tài píng hóu kuí) (see chapter 4) **Huangshan Yingou** (黃山銀鉤 huáng shān yín gōu) **Laozhu Dafang** (老竹大方 lǎo zhú dà fāng)
	RED	**Qimen Hongcha** (祁門紅茶 qí mén hóng chá) (see chapter 4)
JIANGSU	GREEN	**Dongting Biluochun** (洞庭碧螺春 dòng tíng bì luó chūn) (see chapter 4) **Nanjing Rain Flower Tea** (南京雨花茶 nán jīng yǔ huā chá) **Jintan Queshe** (金壇雀舌 jīn tán què shé) **Qianfeng Xuelian** (前峰雪蓮 qián fēng xuě lián)
ZHEJIANG	GREEN	**Xihu Longjing** (aka Dragon Well 西湖龍井 xī hú lóng jǐng) (see chapter 4) **Anji Baicha** (安吉白茶 ān jí bái chá) (see chapter 4) **Guzhu Zisun** (顧渚紫筍 gù zhǔ zǐ sǔn) **Huimingcha** (惠明茶 huì míng chá) **Pingshui Zhucha** (平水珠茶 píng shuǐ zhū chá) **Yandang Maofeng** (雁蕩毛峰 yàn dàng máo fēng)
	YELLOW	**Mogan Huangya** (莫干黃芽 mò gàn huáng yá) **Wenzhou Huangtang** (溫州黃湯 wēn zhōu huáng tāng)
	RED	**Yuehong Gongfu** (越紅功夫 yuè hóng gōng fū)

Jiangbei Tea Region

江北茶區 jiāng běi chá qū

Jiangbei, meaning north of the Yangzi River, receives less rain and experiences high temperature differences between day and night. The region specializes in green tea and the climate produces fragrant, rich tea leaves that last multiple brews. Jiangbei consists of parts of Henan, Shaanxi, Gansu, Shandong, Anhui, Jiangsu, and Hubei provinces.

FAMOUS TEAS FROM JIANGBEI

WHERE	TEA TYPE	TEA
SHAANXI	GREEN	**Wuzi Xianhao** (午子仙毫 wǔ zǐ xiān háo) **Ziyang Maojian** (紫陽毛尖 zǐ yáng máo jiān) **Qinba Wuhao** (秦巴霧毫 qín bā wù háo)
HENAN	GREEN	**Xinyang Maojian** (信陽毛尖 xìn yáng máo jiān) (see chapter 4) **Lingshan Jianfeng** (靈山劍峰 líng shān jiàn fēng) **Taibai Yinhao** (太白銀毫 tài bái yín háo)
HUBEI	GREEN	**Shuangqiao Maojian** (雙橋毛尖 shuāng qiáo máo jiān) **Cheyunshan Maojian** (車雲山毛尖 chē yún shān máo jiān) **Guishan Yanlu** (龜山岩綠 guī shān yán lǜ)
SHANDONG	GREEN	**Rizhao Xueqing** (日照雪青 rì zhào xuě qīng)
JIANGSU	GREEN	**Huaguoshan Yunwu** (花果山雲霧 huā guǒ shān yún wù)
ANHUI	GREEN	**Lu'an Guapian** (六安瓜片 lù ān guā piàn) (see chapter 4) **Tianzhu Jianhao** (天柱劍毫 tiān zhù jiàn háo) **Yuexi Cuilan** (岳西翠蘭 yuè xī cuì lán)

TAIWAN

Taiwan is known for its green, wulong and red teas. Pretty much the entirety of Taiwan is invested in tea growing and tea making, but the best-known tea regions are often associated with a specific tea type. Here are some of the most highly regarded Taiwanese tea regions.

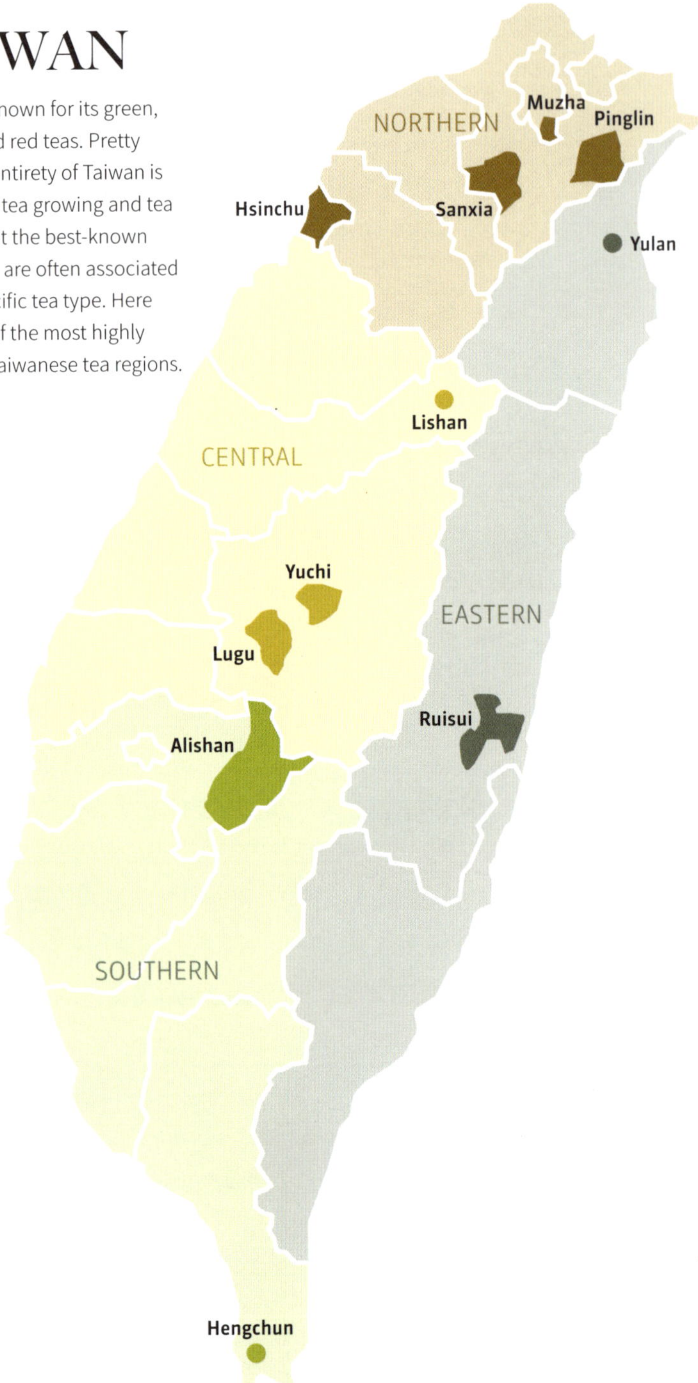

Northern Taiwan

Pinglin

坪林 píng lín

In Taiwan's tea industry there is a saying that goes: South Wulong, North Baozhong (南烏龍北包種 nán wū lóng běi bāo zhǒng). The North refers to the Pinglin tea region in Taipei, which is renowned for its refreshing and fragrant Baozhong (包種 bāo zhǒng), a lightly oxidized wulong tea. Pinglin boasts a long tea-making history, dating back more than 200 years, when tea farmers from mainland China brought their know-how across the straits.

Sanxia

三峽 sān xiá

Sanxia, Taipei, is the only tea region in Taiwan that specializes in green tea, and in particular, Longjing Fangcha ("Longjing-style tea" 龍井仿茶 lóng jǐng fǎng chá). The leaves are picked from local variety Qingxin Ganzai (青心柑仔 qīng xīn gān zǎi), which is found only in Sanxia. Sanxia green tea is crisp and fresh, leaving a pleasant bittersweet aftertaste. While there are excellent green teas in Sanxia, Taiwan is much more renowned for its wulong teas.

Muzha

木柵 mù zhà

Muzha, Taipei, is the birthplace of Taiwanese Tieguanyin (鐵觀音 tiě guān yīn) and boasts over 200 years of history in producing this popular style of wulong tea. Muzha Tieguanyin is quite strong and has a signature tinge of acidity.

Hsinchu

新竹 xīn zhú

Beipu (北埔 běi pǔ) and Emei (峨眉 é méi) townships, both in Hsinchu county, specialize in Oriental Beauty (東方美人 dōng fāng měi rén) — which is only found in Taiwan and is possibly the most treasured of all Taiwanese teas.

WHERE	TEA TYPE	TEA
PINGLIN	WULONG	**Wenshan Baozhong** (文山包種 wén shān bāo zhǒng) (see chapter 4)
SANXIA	GREEN	**Longjing Fangcha** (龍井仿茶 lóng jǐng fǎng chá)
MUZHA	WULONG	**Tieguanyin** (鐵觀音 tiě guān yīn) (see chapter 4)
HSINCHU	WULONG	**Oriental Beauty** (東方美人 dōng fāng měi rén) (see chapter 4)

A tea plantation in Pinglin

Central Taiwan

Yuchi

魚池 yú chí

Yuchi in Nantou county (南投 nán tóu) is home to the famous Sun Moon Lake (日月潭 rì yuè tán), which is known in the tea world for its smooth and complex red tea. The Japanese began to experiment with growing tea in various Taiwanese regions while Taiwan was under Japanese rule from 1895 to 1945, and they discovered that Yuchi's climate and humidity resulted in the perfect red tea.

Lugu

鹿谷 lù gǔ

Lugu in Nantou county enjoys consistent temperatures all year round, as well as soil that retains moisture, helping tea shrubs thrive during winter and spring. The Dongding Wulong (凍頂烏龍 dòng dǐng wū lóng) produced there is one of the most famous tea styles in Taiwan.

Lishan

梨山 lí shān

Lishan in the city of Taichung (台中 tái zhōng) is the highest-altitude tea region in Taiwan, averaging 2,000 meters above sea level. Teas made in Lishan are classified as Gaoshancha (aka High Mountain Tea). The area is cold, especially during winter and spring, and experiences a large daily temperature difference, resulting in fat, nutritious and flavorful tea leaves. Spring harvest takes place usually in May, a month later than other tea regions. With only two harvesting seasons, teas from Lishan are limited and often fetch a higher price.

WHERE	TEA TYPE	TEA
YUCHI	RED	**Sun Moon Lake Red Tea** (日月潭紅茶 rì yuè tán hóng chá) (see chapter 4)
LISHAN	WULONG	**Gaoshancha** (aka High Mountain Tea 高山茶 gāo shān chá) (see chapter 4)
LUGU	WULONG	**Dongding Wulong** (凍頂烏龍 dòng dǐng wū lóng) (see chapter 4)

Southern Taiwan

Alishan

阿里山 ā lǐ shān

Alishan teas, produced in Chiayi county (嘉義 jiā yì), is one of the most highly regarded Gaoshanchas (aka High Mountain Teas) in Taiwan. As the mountains of Alishan are cold and covered in fog, the tea trees are exposed to only short periods of sunshine, minimizing their bitter taste. The tea trees also grow slower, resulting in softer and more tender leaves. Alishan tea is often said to be able to transport the drinker straight to the mountains, with its distinctive Shantouqi ("mountain essence" 山頭氣 shān tóu qì).

Hengchun

恆春 héng chūn

Hengchun is located in Pingtung county (屏東 píng dōng) at the southernmost tip of Taiwan and is home to Taiwan's lowest-altitude teas. Gangkoucha ("harbor tea" 港口茶 gǎng kǒu chá) is truly one-of-a-kind, being full-bodied and with very strong and bitter flavors. As the tea shrubs of Hengchun are subjected to sunshine and sea breezes all year round, locals jokingly refer to Gangkoucha as Haiwucha ("sea fog tea" 海霧茶 hǎi wù chá). Traditionally, rolling and roast-drying of the tea leaves are done in the same wok, and depending on the maker, the resulting tea is somewhere between a green tea and a lightly oxidized wulong.

WHERE	TEA TYPE	TEA
ALISHAN	**WULONG**	**Gaoshancha** (aka High Mountain Tea 高山茶 gāo shān chá)
LISHAN	**GREEN / WULONG**	**Gangkoucha** (港口茶 gǎng kǒu chá)

Eastern Taiwan

Yulan

玉蘭 yù lán

As its name suggests, Yulan township in Yilan county (宜蘭 yí lán) is famous for its Yulancha (玉蘭茶 yù lán chá), which includes green, wulong, and red teas made in Yulan. Yilan county is said to be the "backyard of Taiwan" and is known nationally for its clean air and water. Yulan tea is said to possess an especially pure aroma.

Ruisui

瑞穗 ruì suì

Located at the southern edge of Taiwan, Ruisui township, in Hualian county (花蓮 huā lián) was in fact a coffee-producing region during the Japanese occupation. After the Japanese left, Ruisui experimented with growing various crops and made its name when its Tianhecha (天鶴茶 tiān hè chá), a red tea with strong honey notes, won praises across Taiwan. It is now the biggest tea region in Hualian.

Besides Ruisui, Hualian county is generally known for its red teas. The most popular red tea cultivar in the region is the Daiye Wulong (大葉烏龍 dà yè wū lóng), which is beloved for its strong honey notes.

WHERE	TEA TYPE	TEA
YULAN	**GREEN / WULONG / RED**	**Yulancha** (玉蘭茶 yù lán chá)
RUISUI	**WULONG / RED**	Luye (鹿野 lù yě) **Tianhecha** (天鶴茶 tiān hè chá)

TEA ETIQUETTE

How do you brew a proper cup of tea? The simplest answer to this question is to pour some boiling water into a pot of tea leaves. Voila. Life's too short to make things any more complicated.

But of course, if you want to be more formal about your tea appreciation, if you want to socialize with your guests while you make a pot of your prized tea, or if you want to turn tea drinking into an art form (and even meditate on it), then there are plenty of ways to up your game. Here are some general guidelines that you may or may not want to follow the next time you make some tea for yourself or friends at home.

A typical tea set on a bamboo tea tray: tea leaf holder, pitcher (aka fairness cup), gaiwan, teacups, and some bamboo utensils

TEAWARE

Serious tea drinkers might have a full set of custom tea furniture made to suit their needs, but for the rest of us, some tea cups and a teapot will probably do.

Typical teaware sets that you'll be able to find at the shops will include four to six small cups, a teapot that fits in one's palm, and a pitcher. The fancier ones might come with a slotted tea tray, usually made out of bamboo, to allow for some excitingly messy pouring. This general combo is what we would recommend as your basic tea appreciation kit.

The teapot and tea cups are usually small and dainty because good teas are meant to be brewed multiple times and enjoyed in small batches. It is said that great teas can easily withstand a dozen steeps, and each steep is meant to be unique. General consensus is that the fourth to fifth brews are the best — the unique character of the tea would have had time to shine through by then, with eventual dilution still held at bay. Of course, there are plenty of exceptions to this rule.

The pitcher, also known as a fairness cup (公道杯 **gōng dào bēi**), is to ensure that all tea drinkers experience exactly the same flavors. The tea made in the teapot is poured first into the pitcher — liquid only; leaves stay in the pot. The tea is then poured from pitcher to each cup. If the tea was to go from teapot (where the tea leaves are held and brewed) straight to each cup, the first cup would theoretically be the mildest and the last cup would be the strongest, since some time would have passed between the first pour and the last pour. The pitcher eliminates this problem.

There are also tea-handling utensils that you can purchase to make life easier. Usually the utensils are sold as a set consisting of a bamboo holding vessel (茶筒 **chá tǒng**); a scoop (茶則 **chá zé**) to grab the tea leaves; a tea spoon (茶匙 **chá chí**) for sorting and transferring the tea leaves; a tea tong (茶夾 **chá jiā**) to grab the teacups (which can be hot if they have been pre-heated); and a tea pick (茶針 **chá zhēn**) to clear the leaves that clog the teapot spout.

A gaiwan (蓋碗 **gài wǎn**) — essentially a large teacup with a saucer and lid — can stand in for a teapot but will require slightly more advanced pouring skills. You simply put the tea leaves into the gaiwan, fill it with boiling water, then close the lid. When you're ready to pour, wrap your thumb and middle finger around the rim of the gaiwan and press your index finger on top of the nub on the lid to keep the tea leaves from falling out — all while maintaining the smallest of slits between lid and cup to allow the water to stream out. It's not as complicated as it sounds, but does require practice!

For drinkers of Pu'er, there is also a tea knife (茶刀 **chá dāo**) that can be used to break apart the tightly pressed tea cakes.

YIXING ZISHA

If you're looking to up your tea brewing game, many tea aficionados swear by Yixing zisha teapots ("purple clay pot" 宜興紫砂壺 yí xìng zǐ shā hú), adored for the way they improve a tea's textures and aromas. Think of it as music lovers preferring vinyl over digital recordings. Zisha is a famous type of clay from the city of Yixing in Jiangsu Province. The clay's porous nature allows it to absorb the oils of the tea leaves after each brew, and over time, the teapot itself is said to develop its own distinctive flavors. The zisha material also has excellent heat-retaining properties.

Yixing teapots are definitely investment pieces. It's recommended that a Yixing teapot be used for only one type or specific style of tea. It will take many brews before a Yixing teapot becomes saturated with a tea's particular aroma — but once it does, you've hit tea-drinking jackpot.

When shopping for a Yixing teapot, research beforehand in order to determine what size, shape and clay type best suits your tea-drinking needs. For instance, a thin-skinned teapot with a smaller opening is best for more aromatic teas such as green, white and wulong. A thicker, more porous pot with a larger opening is more suited to less aromatic, larger-leaf teas such as red and Pu'er tea.

CERAMIC & PORCELAIN

Glazed ceramic (陶瓷 táo cí) and porcelain (白瓷 bái cí) teawares are impermeable and flavor-neutral. They do not affect or absorb flavors in any way. Most standard teaware sets on the market are made from ceramic or porcelain.

Jingdezhen (景德鎮 jǐng dé zhèn) in Jiangxi province is known as the Porcelain Capital, and this town has been specializing in pottery-making for over 1,700 years. Today, Jingdezhen is known for producing durable, thin-walled, and beautifully crafted porcelain wares.

DID YOU KNOW?

Celadon (青瓷 qīng cí) or greenware, a special type of jade-green pottery covered in a cracked transparent glaze, is another popular material for teaware.

Jian Zhan (建盏 jiàn zhǎn) stoneware from Fujian province, which boasts a rainbow-like sheen, is also proving to be a hit with today's young tea drinkers.

HOW MUCH TEA?

The stronger you like your tea, the more tea leaves you should use and the longer you should steep your tea. That's our unofficial advice anyhow.

For most teas, the official rule of thumb is that you can fill up to one fifth or sixth of your cup or teapot with dried tea leaves, and the rest with water. That's roughly about 6 to 8 grams of dried leaves per small Chinese teapot. High-quality tea leaves can withstand at least half a dozen steeps or brews at a time. We use the terms "steep" and "brew" interchangeably here: both describe the act of mixing tea leaves in hot water for a set period of time.

THE FIRST "RINSE"

For many of the darker-colored teas, it's generally recommended that you immediately pour out the first steep to "rinse off" any dirt particles that came with the dried tea leaves, and to "open up" the tea.

If you're brewing your tea in a pot, then all you need to do is pour boiling water onto the tea leaves, swirl the pot a little, and pour the water straight out again. This is when a tea tray can come in handy, since any excess water can be poured right through the slits of the tray cover and collected in the tray container.

BREWING TEMPERATURES AND TIMES

If you're drinking a light-colored tea like white or green tea, typical advice is to use slightly-lower-than-boiling-temperature water (80 degrees Celsius or thereabouts) to brew your drink. The reasoning is that light-colored, minimally processed teas are more delicate and are more susceptible to being "ruined" by too-hot water.

Dark-colored teas like red tea and black tea, on the other hand, can withstand the hotter temperatures, so pouring boiling water (95 degrees Celsius and up) straight onto the tea leaves won't pose a problem.

In short, the temperature of the hot water you use is dependent on the perceived strength of the tea, strength being directly related to the tea type. Having said this, we are not exactly encouraging any of our readers to purchase a thermometer and inadvertently turn their tea-drinking experience into a scientific experiment. Put some boiling water aside for a few minutes if you want to cool it down, and it works just as well as any fancy measuring tool.

Another rule to remember is that the hotter the water, the shorter amount of time you'll need to steep a tea for the flavors to come through. The colder the water, the longer it'll take. You can steep your tea anywhere from 30 seconds to a few minutes at a time. After the first few steeps, you can add 20 to 30 seconds to each additional steep, since the tea leaves do get diluted over time.

And finally, the better quality your tea, the more steeps it can handle. Some of the best teas out there can withstand up to dozens of steeps!

GO WITH THE FLOW

For serious tea drinkers, the way one pours water into the teapot can affect the tea's taste. There are three general methods of pouring:

Gentle ("gentle steep" 溫潤泡 wēn rùn pào): Hold a kettle of boiling water not too high from the teapot or gaiwan where the tea leaves are held. Pour water slowly around the rim of the pot, spiralling inwards. This gentle style is suitable for black teas like Shu Pu'er.

Concentrated ("high pour narrow stream" 高沖細流 gāo chōng xì liú): Hold the kettle higher, and aim a narrow stream of water around the rim and on the leaves, spiralling inwards and stopping at the center. This style is suitable for bringing out the flavors of teas like wulong.

Cyclone ("fixed point rapid current" 定點激流 dìng diǎn jī liú): Hold the kettle at a diagonal angle (from the 4 o'clock position in relation to the teapot or gaiwan), and move the kettle up and down while pouring. This will produce a cyclone effect and "excite" the tea leaves. This method is suitable for green teas and for rinsing teas.

CUPS ONLY?

Some green tea drinkers like to use a big glass cup to steep their tea — teapots be banished. You can technically do the same for any tea with good-looking tea leaves that can benefit from a full viewing (as opposed to being hidden in a teapot). With darker-colored teas, using a teapot is the more common default.

SHAPE MATTERS

With wulong teas, the recommended leaf-to-water ratio as well as steep time is highly dependent on the shape of the leaves. For instance, Anxi Tieguanyin tea leaves are tightly curled into tiny balls and have the capacity to expand quite a bit more than loose-leaf teas once steeped in water. Which means one can either put less tea leaves or put more water into the pot when brewing an Anxi Tieguanyin.

Steeping time for the first brew is also generally longer than the standard 30 seconds, since the curled-up leaves need more time to open up. Subsequent steeps can follow standard procedure.

A cup of Shu Pu'er with some char siu bao (steamed barbecue pork buns) during dim sum
Photo: Alan Pang

THE ART OF TEA PAIRING

Tea goes with pretty much everything, as far as we're concerned!

In many Chinese restaurants, teas are served as the default beverage rather than water. No matter what dishes are ordered, the assumption is that tea would be the perfect companion. Typically, the staff would give patrons a selection of tea styles to choose from, and then a fully brewed pot would sit on the table for the whole group to enjoy during the meal. At fancier establishments, each patron might be able to choose their own individually served tea.

Generally speaking, "tea pairing" isn't really a thing in Chinese culture beyond the fact that tea is served with anything and everything edible. But the Chinese do have fast and loose rules when it comes to which teas are more suitable for different seasons of the year, as well as for different body types and conditions. This all ties back to tea's intricate link with Traditional Chinese Medicine, which borrows from Yin Yang theory and the Five Elements philosophy and all that those two worldviews entail. More on this in a bit!

Tea drinkers in general are getting more sophisticated when it comes to what they consume, and the world of artisanal tea is also evolving to accommodate their demands. One prominent result: high-end restaurants have started to create tea-pairing menus similar in concept to wine pairings, and tea sommeliers are becoming a more and more common sight.

Despite these developments in the artisanal tea arena, there are some traditional Chinese tea drinkers who still believe that Chinese tea is best left alone — that is, it does not need to and should not be paired with food. To these purists, tea should be drunk on its own, and the best times to indulge are before and after a meal. In short, the thinking is that tea should be appreciated as is, rather than as an accompaniment to food.

Furthermore, most traditional tea masters will advise against having food alongside your tea. Many tea books recommend only drinking tea half an hour before or after a meal, and never at the same time as your meal. When it comes to tea appreciation, the idea is to keep your taste buds pure to truly experience the tea.

On the other hand, tea has always been a culinary experience throughout Chinese history. In the Tang dynasty, Chazhou ("tea congee" 茶粥 chá zhōu) was a food item that consisted of rice mixed with tea leaves and ginger. Meanwhile, the Chinese Hakka favor a cereal-like Leicha (擂茶 léi chá) tea paste that is more solid than liquid, while the Miao people consume a savory Youcha ("oil tea" 油茶 yóu chá) tea-based dish that incorporates deep-fried peanuts, sticky rice and corn. The people of Guangdong and Hong Kong famously enjoy their dim sum along with cups and cups of sizzling hot tea.

The point is that there is no one right way to enjoy your tea. If pairing tea with food makes your meal more enjoyable, then why not?

Out of the Spotlight

When exploring tea pairing options, the tea no longer takes priority — it's all about finding what works best together between food and drink. And that sometimes means sacrificing common tea rituals (see chapter 6) and just going along with the flow of the meal.

Getting Prepared

The traditional method of making multiple brews for a chosen style of tea works when you're enjoying only one style of tea at a time. You can enjoy multiple brews without bringing disruption to the meal.

But if you're pairing a tea with a particular main course or dish, difficulties can arise. One recommendation is to prepare the best brew of a chosen tea just before serving each course. Very generally speaking, wulong teas are usually most fragrant by the third or fourth steep, while Pu'er teas are the richest by the fifth or sixth steep.

It's best to include the tea brewing process into your meal preparation and to make the desired brew right before you serve each designated dish.

How Much Tea?

As previously mentioned, the traditional method of tea brewing results in multiple steeps and a lengthy tea drinking experience. When it comes to tea pairing, this doesn't have to be the case. The focus of a meal would naturally be on the food, and what goes well with it. There may be multiple courses and multiple pairings, and a diner might only experience several sips of a tea per dish as a result.

Hot or Cold?

Most traditional tea drinkers would find cold tea appalling, but tea pairing is all about being creative and finding new combinations that complement each other. Imagine a cold and refreshing glass of tea with your carpaccio, or a chilly and rich Pu'er with a light and soft cheese — sounds pretty tempting to us. You can even carbonate your cold brew and make sparkling teas. But for chocolate desserts, a hot red tea might be a more pleasurable match. The sky's the limit, in other words!

PAIRING GUIDELINES

Pairing suggestions given by:

May Chan
HOMELAND TEA GARDEN

Ann Sit
FOOK MING TONG

Nana Chan
PLANTATION TEAS

Catherine Yung
YÚ TEAHOUSE

Like Attracts Like

As a very general — but easily breakable — rule of thumb, stronger flavored teas will pair more naturally with more intensely flavored dishes.

It's also no coincidence that darker-colored teas tend to be perceived as stronger flavored than their lighter-hued counterparts, and while this is a convenient way to make fast judgment, you'll most definitely find exceptions. How one defines "stronger", for instance, can be very different from individual to individual. Some might very well find the grassiness of a light-colored tea a more defining characteristic than a nutty red tea. Also, sometimes dishes with very rich flavors will clash with instead of complement a very rich style of tea, and vice versa.

In short: the best way to know for sure is to taste the tea before making any decisions!

By Cooking Method

The way a dish is prepared can determine what type of tea is generally more suitable to go along with it. For instance, a lightly steamed dish with minimal seasoning calls for a lighter-style tea for pairing purposes. On the opposite end of the spectrum, deep-fried foods or dishes that are heavily spiced might be better suited for a tea that can hold its own.

By Ingredient Type

Savory Foods

RED MEAT

Red meat like beef, lamb and pork or generally fattier meat can pair with equally rich teas like Shu Pu'er, which is said to be able to cut through the grease and also act as a proper (non-alcoholic) digestif.

Wuyi Yancha, a strong and smoky style of wulong, is another suitable choice for heavy dishes like grilled meats.

Beyond Food

Historically, tea not only appeared in restaurants, but also in music venues and Xiqu (Chinese opera) houses. It was a popular beverage for creative minds like renowned Tang dynasty poet Bai Juyi.

Today, there are many non-food-related tea pairing options available: think cigars, yoga, and fragrances paired with tea!

WHITE MEAT

Seafood, poultry and white meat, which are generally considered leaner than red meat, can go well with a wulong like a light Tieguanyin. Seafood especially is said to be a good match with white teas.

Relatively speaking, any type of meat is still considered as "heavier" than any non-meat-based ingredient, so a Shu Pu'er could also technically be a good companion to lean meat.

VEGETABLES

Fresh vegetables go especially well with a light-colored tea for its more refreshing qualities. Anything too rich can overwhelm the native flavors of a lightly prepared vegetable dish.

NUTS

Nuts, with their distinctively "nutty" (for lack of a better word!) flavor profiles, are a natural match for something with more intensity, like a red tea. Some green teas, which naturally have notes of toasted nuts, also work well.

DIM SUM / SAVORY SNACKS

Dim sum dishes, afternoon tea snacks, and tapas come in all shapes and flavors, so it's hard to find one tea that matches them all. But it doesn't hurt to choose one main focal point of the meal, and then to find a tea that goes with it.

Something complex like a multi-textured and multi-flavored barbecued pork char siu pastry can go with a similarly complex, multi-layered wulong. Something with a tangy note (like a dish that contains lemon) would be well complemented by a strong and acidic red tea.

Sweet Foods

CHOCOLATES / CREAMY TREATS

Chocolates themselves occupy a whole flavor spectrum from treacly sweet to intensely bitter, but generally speaking, milk chocolates and other creamy treats make a good case for a cup of floral or fruity wulong. Meanwhile, a sophisticated dark chocolate can be paired with a strong, dark-roasted wulong.

FRUITY DISHES

This might be a no-brainer but fruity treats will be a natural match for teas with fruity notes (which span the entire tea spectrum).

By Different Seasons

First things first: of course you're allowed to drink whatever tea you darn well feel like, whenever you want. We're not here to set arbitrary rules or to make things unnecessarily complicated. But sometimes there are situations that make one type of tea more or less suitable for the occasion, and that's what we're here to help point out.

Some of these guidelines are simple and common-sense-based, while some lean on Traditional Chinese Medicine theory, which ascribes health-related functions and properties to anything that's edible or potable.

Generally speaking, the warmer and hotter months of the year warrant lighter and fruitier teas, while the cooler and colder months call for teas that are more robust and strong in flavor.

The teas are, of course, always consumed hot — at least traditionally speaking. So whether it's sweltering or freezing outside, you're supposed to keep your kettle boiling. Side note: bubble tea shops around the world are about to change this tradition for good.

Spring / Summer

Teas are assigned inherent Hanliang ("cooling" 寒涼 hán liáng) or Shanghuo ("heaty" 上火 shàng huǒ) properties, according to Traditional Chinese Medicine. For instance, lightly processed teas like green tea and white tea are said to be more cooling for the body, and therefore appropriate for spring and summer. Conveniently, green and white teas are also perceived to be more mild in flavor.

Fall / Winter

Meanwhile, more heavily processed teas like red tea and black tea (fermented tea) — which also happen to be more aggressive on the flavor spectrum — are said to be more Shanghuo and therefore more fall- and winter-friendly.

Other types of tea, like wulong, are harder to pinpoint, since depending on their style and production method they can fall on either the cooler or warmer end of the spectrum. But a safe gauge would be to look at the color of the brew — the darker it is, the more inherently warming and strong it likely is, and hence the more suitable it would be during the colder seasons. It's definitely not rocket science!

By Health Conditions

Everything to do with food and drink can be traced back to Traditional Chinese Medicine and its roots in Yin Yang and the Five Elements theory. This especially includes Chinese tea, which was originally viewed as a medicinal herb and was treated as such when it was first discovered thousands of years ago, before tea drinking became more widespread.

Delving into the intricacies of Traditional Chinese Medicine is beyond the scope of this book, but it would be irresponsible of us to not mention its influence on the way the Chinese drink and treat their teas.

Tea is inherently seen as a cold ingredient — it lands on the Yin spectrum of things. Although, since there are always exceptions, red teas are actually classified as mildly hot. Clear as mud, we know.

For sensitive souls, some tea experts and Chinese Medicine practitioners suggest: avoiding tea at night in case its caffeine content affects one's sleep; and steeping one's tea for a shorter period of time to enjoy a gentler version of the drink.

Feeling Hot?

Traditional Chinese Medicine alleges that people get sick when their body is out of balance, or when there is too much Yin or Yang in their systems. Having too much heat, or Shanghuo (上火 **shàng huǒ**), usually results in symptoms like a sore throat, insomnia, pimples and constipation. In situations like these, brewing a tea that has inherently cold properties to bring the body back to balance is considered an appropriate home remedy. Green tea, for instance, is said to reduce internal heat, promote the production of body fluids and tone down inflammation.

Feeling Cold?

If you naturally have cold hands and feet, you're likely to be on the cold Yin end of the spectrum, or Hanliang (寒涼 **hán liáng**). It's generally not advisable for you to drink green tea since it is also considered as inherently cold by TCM standards. "Warm" teas such as red tea and Pu'er are believed to help promote circulation and warmth in the body.

Indigestion

Suffering from indigestion? More heavily oxidized teas such as wulong and black tea (fermented tea) are said to be great for one's digestive health. Those with a sensitive stomach should stay away from frequent consumption of green tea, since it is supposedly harsher on the digestive system.

These are just general guidelines on what types of tea match well with different bodily needs, but ultimately, most tea experts stress the importance of listening to your body. Use these guidelines as a reference, but take note to observe how your body responds to the teas that you drink.

Learn to tell if you're Chazui ("tea drunk" 茶醉 chá zuì), a term that experts use to describe the adverse effects of drinking too much tea. The most common signs are an upset stomach, heart palpitations and a headache.

By contrast, a tea that works well with your body will make you feel awesome on the inside and may even cause a burp or two!

What Gives Tea Its Flavors?

POLYPHENOLS

Polyphenols are natural compounds that are found in the tea leaf, and include tannins, which are known for their astringency. The more a tea is oxidized, the less polyphenols it contains. This is why green tea is more astringent than wulong or red tea.

CAFFEINE

The stimulant caffeine gives tea a slightly bitter taste. Caffeine is believed to be the most stable compound in a tea leaf and is thus least affected by processing. There is no established correlation between tea type and caffeine content. The tea cultivar itself and the terroir can affect caffeine levels, according to Taiwanese tea researchers.

THEANINE

Theanine is a type of amino acid found in tea leaves. Theanine gives tea its fragrance and sweetness, and is perceived to have a relaxant effect.

CARBOHYDRATES

Carbohydrates such as fructose and glucose contribute to a tea's sweetness. Oxidation breaks down tea polyphenols into carbohydrates, which is why heavily oxidized wulong and red teas are noticeably sweeter than green teas.

ORGANIC ACID

Tea leaves also contain a small amount of organic acid, which gives the tea a slightly tangy flavor. There is usually more organic acid in a heavily oxidized tea such as wulong and red tea.

AROMA COMPOUNDS

Lightly oxidized teas like green tea generally contain less aroma compounds than more heavily oxidized teas like red tea.

THE TEA MAKERS

Although most consumers purchase their teas from stores and big retailers, sometimes the best way to ensure a high-quality product is to go straight to the tea makers themselves. These are the people who manage the tea fields every day; who help to harvest the tea leaves during tea season; who transform the fresh green leaves into dried tea leaves; who make calculations and adjustments depending on the harvest and the weather; and who package and then distribute the tea or even sell directly to consumers. These are the artisans who dedicate their lives to the art of making tea. During our research for this book, we've had the pleasure of meeting many of these amazing tea experts — and here are some of their stories.

THE LEGACY HOLDER

Wilson Hsu's family owns several large tea fields as well as a tea shop in Hsinchu, Taiwan, specializing in Oriental Beauty tea (a heavily oxidized style of wulong). The family's expertise is renowned: their teas have won the top prize at the twice-yearly tea competition in their county more than a dozen times since 1997. Like most small-scale tea plantations, the Hsu family manages the entire tea production process. Wilson is a fourth generation tea maker, having taken over the business from his father.

When Wilson travels around Asia to meet with potential distributors, he usually starts with explaining the special position a particular insect occupies in his work. "Without the Jacobiasca formosana (小綠葉蟬 xiǎo lǜ yè chán), there is no Oriental Beauty tea," he declares. The green-colored insect, part of the leafhopper family and no bigger than the size of a flea, loves to bite and feast on the tea leaves, kickstarting the oxidation process, Hsu explains — and this in turn gives the tea leaves a striking sweetness that defines the Oriental Beauty style.

"We tea farmers are nature's servants. These leafhoppers are picky. We use only natural fertilizers. If we don't take care of our tea fields,

the leafhoppers might not come back next year," Wilson says.

For Oriental Beauty tea makers, harvesting begins in the early hours of the day and runs into the afternoon, and then processing begins and continues late into the night. Because Oriental Beauty is a heavily oxidized tea, the drying and shaping stages are carefully repeated every hour for 24 hours to produce the desired results. "During tea season, we don't get much sleep at all for a couple of weeks. Throughout the night, we perform make-green on the tea leaves and decide on what else needs to be done, depending on the moisture and aroma level of the leaves," Wilson says. "The most horrifying part is that you cannot be certain of the batch's quality until you actually have the finished tea."

Wilson belongs to an increasingly common crop of young third or fourth-generation Taiwanese tea makers taking on the family business. "It is exhausting, but once I started learning, I fell completely in love," he says. "It is extremely rewarding. We begin with fresh leaves that have almost no flavor at all. But throughout the process, the leaves transform and generate this seductive sweetness. This astounds me and keeps me going, every time."

THE BROTHERS WHO CHANGED THEIR MINDS

Jacob Bai and his brother are fifth generation tea makers from a renowned family in Pinglin, Taiwan, that specializes in Wenshan Baozhong, a lightly oxidized strip-shaped wulong. Growing up, the brothers had no intention of taking over the business. "We had to help out during the tea harvests when we were kids," Jacob says. "And it was really tough. Everyone was grumpy and we worked all day. I wanted to get as far away from the business as possible, and I did."

"But one day some years ago, my brother casually asked me what was going to happen to the tea plantations," Jacob says. That was when it dawned on the brothers that their father was getting older and could not carry on forever. Learning the craft of tea-making was

surprisingly challenging for the brothers. "For some reason, once my dad talked in tea-speak, I didn't understand a single word he said. I clearly wasn't paying attention back in the day," Jacob recalls.

Wenshan Baozhong is considered a light tea, known for its floral and milky notes. "At first, I just memorized all the different tasting notes. It took me around four years to truly develop my palate," he says.

Once the brothers decided to take over, they revamped the entire business model as well. The Bai family used to sell most of their finished tea to wholesalers. "My father works really hard to make tea, and we wanted to tell that story," Jacob says. "So we started our own brand, designed our own packaging and opened social media accounts. We sell most of our teas directly to the consumers now."

While finding the labor to help harvest and process the tea leaves is getting increasingly difficult, as young people are reluctant to join the physically demanding industry, Jacob sees pollution and urban development as their biggest challenges. "Tea is closely tied to the environment. Any change in the soil and water quality is reflected in the tea," he says. "We're seeing more fluctuations in the weather and also more urban developments, which lead to pollution. If the environment deteriorates, the tea deteriorates."

THE ECO-FARMER

Chen Luho's family has been making tea in Pinglin, Taiwan for four generations, but instead of taking up his family business, Mr. Chen decided to work as an engineer. His family's tea business consequently closed down. When he retired 13 years ago at 50 years old, Mr. Chen had a change of heart, went back to his roots, and started an eco-tea farm. "Pinglin is my home. When I learned about the pollution the tea industry and other industries were inflicting on the environment, I wanted to protect the area," Mr. Chen says. "I wanted to show that there was a sustainable way of tea making going forward."

Mr. Chen rented several abandoned tea plots in Pinglin, and began the arduous process of turning the fields into eco-certified ones. "It takes three years of eco-farming before the land is officially certified, as it takes time for previous pesticides and fertilizers to dissipate." The hard work paid off when Mr. Chen noticed that the near-threatened emerald tea frog (翡翠綠蛙 fěi cuì lǜ wā), which was said to have disappeared from Pinglin, started visiting his plantations. "It tells me that the ecosystem is more diversified, and I'm closer to achieving ecological balance in my fields," he says. "If managed carefully, development and the environment can go hand in hand."

Organic tea, however, is not as highly regarded, Mr. Chen admits. "We do not use any pesticides and artificial fertilizers, which means the resulting tea leaves often have breakage and are not standardized," he says. "Organic tea stands no chance in competitions because judges are looking for evenly shaped leaves. I do hope this perception will one day change."

THE CULTURAL AMBASSADOR

About a three-hour drive from Jinghong city in Yunnan, Weng Jing (翁景 **wēng jǐng**) is a historic village situated at the highest peak of Jingmai Mountain in Xishuangbanna, near Pu'er City — an area that's famous for its eponymously named tea. At the local village temple, Myanmar is visible from across the mountains. Most of the villagers here belong to the Bulang minority ethnic group, for which tea has always been a big part of their everyday life.

"When I was growing up, tea was not seen as a specialty craft or a potential career," says 31-year-old tea maker San Wen. "It was just something that every family had and produced on their own, a way to make the best out of what nature provides, as there are so many tea trees in the area. People drink it throughout the day and especially when there are guests. My grandma always harvests and makes her own tea."

In 2013, San Wen partnered up with his older brother and cousin to launch their own tea brand. He estimates that the trees in his tea fields are 800 to 900 years old. "Because Pu'er tea is so important to Bulang culture, we chose that as the basis of our business — the thing we

will work hard for, for the rest of our lives," he says. "Our culture believes in spirit. In tea, we call it tea soul (茶魂 **chá hún**). Why does Sheng Pu'er tea change every year? Because its soul is still around. The honey notes from the first years turn into an orchid floral note after several years. Life is fragile, but even if something is dead, its spirit stays with us."

San Wen makes a wide range of tea at his plantation, including white tea, red tea and Pu'er. He believes in growing tea the natural way, avoiding pesticides and artificial fertilizers. To diversify the ecosystem and for an additional source of income, he also keeps bees and sells honey. "I am very worried about these natural resources — there are so many development opportunities like opening up restaurants. And once pollution kicks in, the forest deteriorates and the tea making will be over," he says. "It's easy for my generation — we'll be gone before that happens. But what will it be like for my sons' generation if we don't protect these trees now? That's why we need to develop in a sustainable manner."

William Osmont and wife Yubai
Photo: Farmerleaf

THE CONNOISSEUR

Originally from France, William Osmont now lives in Jingmai, Yunnan and runs a tea brand and shop with his Yunnan-born wife, Yubai. After graduating from high school, he spent a year in China to learn the language and to explore Yunnan's tea mountains. He then studied agricultural engineering in France and tea science in Taiwan. The husband-and-wife duo grows and processes their own Sheng Pu'er tea, and also sources teas from other small-scale farmers. "We sell mostly Sheng Pu'er, only very little Shu Pu'er," he says. "People who are into Pu'er usually prefer Sheng Pu'er, because there is much more variety — there are so many different mountains to explore."

When it comes to Sheng Pu'er tea, the terroir plays a large role in its resulting flavor. "I'd say Sheng Pu'er is 80 percent terroir, 20 percent processing," he says. "The defining feature of Sheng Pu'er from Jingmai Mountain is its straightforwardness. You have great orchid fragrance, good sweetness and a fast aftertaste."

William is passionate about educating people about tea. "Tea classifications is a big mess," he says. "I believe it more useful to understand the processing steps and what each step does to the tea. That's the thing I like to teach."

As tea farmers, William says much depends on the weather. "If the tea doesn't taste good, then that's that," he says. "For Pu'er tea there's a saying: it's great if you can sell your tea this year, but it's even better if you can't. Because you may be able to sell for a better price next year. So there's no pressure."

THE MULTI-TASKER

Zhu Jianying had married into a tea-making family: the Wengs of Weng Jia Shan (翁家山 **wēng jiā shān**), a tea village near Longjing in Hangzhou where most households have been tea makers for generations. For most of the year, she actually spends her time as a private driver. "Authentic Longjing tea is harvested and processed only once a year during spring, to ensure its quality. Those several weeks are very stressful," she says. "Other times, it's boring to be trapped at home, you know? I'd rather be outside meeting new people and seeing new things."

Tea season typically begins in late March and ends in mid-April, just before the summer rain hits. During this period, the village is swamped with visitors. "You can barely walk down the streets. There'll be tea pickers, tourists, buyers…" Ms. Zhu says. "Every household will be making tea. The whole family has to chip in. You'll see us kill-greening just in our front yard. It's a sight to behold." Early to mid- harvests are turned into Longjing green tea, while some of the later plucks are processed into a red tea called Jiuqu Hongmei ("nine tunes red plums" 九曲紅梅 **jiǔ qū hóng méi**).

It's early March when we speak to her, and the entire village is anxiously awaiting the upcoming tea season. "This once-a-year tea season is extremely important for the entire village. We're checking on the tea plants every day, hoping they grow slowly and nicely," she says. "If it suddenly gets warm and then cold again, we'll get weaker buds and leaves, and that means trouble for the whole year. Right now, all we can do is hope."

THE TRAILBLAZER

Anji Baicha, a green tea from Anji county in Zhejiang province, is a relatively new style in the history of Chinese tea. It's a great case study in how a tea can become popular in society when the right factors are in place. "When I was growing up, the area was lined with mostly bamboo farms or forests," second-generation tea maker Liang Minjie from Kuntong, Anji recalls. "Now, most households grow tea."

When the Anji Baicha cultivar was discovered around 30 years ago, more locals went into tea farming, but it wasn't until a national enterprise consolidated some of the biggest tea farms and diverted resources into establishing distribution channels and marketing that Anji Baicha became better known around China. "We work mostly with bigger brands, on top of selling directly to consumers," Mr. Liang says. "They are able to reach customers that we small farmers won't be able to."

Liang's family is one of the most respected tea makers in the area. "My father cultivated this tea field on the highest peak in Anji 15 years ago," he says. "There wasn't even a road up the mountain. He had to build the road himself, and cultivate and seed the land with his own hands. It didn't make any money for the first five years. To have the determination to do one thing and to do it well — that is what I strive for as a tea maker."

GLOSSARY

REFERENCES

Note that even though we used the following books as references, sometimes we found that not all of the information given was consistent or completely accurate. We do not necessarily endorse all of the books we list here.

BOOKS

By Author

王旭烽。茶與茶人。台北：漫遊者文化事業股份有限公司，2016。書籍。

王明祥。茶味裡的隱知識。新北市：幸福文化，2019。書籍。

王建榮。茶道：從喝茶到懂茶。香港：萬里機構・飲食天地出版社，2016。書籍。

安妮・皮埃爾-羅伯特。茶。香港：三聯書店（香港）有限公司，2002。書籍。

池中憲。尋味。中國茶。台北：積木文化，2005。書籍。

於觀亭。觀亭說茶：鑒茶.泡茶.茶藝。山西科學技術出版社，2014。Kindle。

琳達・蓋拉德（Linda Gaylard）。茶。百科。台北：楓書坊，2017。書籍。

蔡榮章。茶道・基礎篇-泡茶原理與應用。台北：武陵出版有限公司，2003，書籍。

d'Offay, Timothy. Easy Leaf Tea. Ryland Peters & Small, 2017. Print.

Gebely, Tony. Tea: A User's Guide. Chicago: Eggs and Toast Media, LLC, 2016. Kindle edition.

Peltier, Warren. Ancient Art of Tea: Wisdom From the Ancient Chinese Tea Master. Vermont: Tuttle Publishing, 2011. Kindle Edition.

Souter, Keith. The Tea Cyclopedia: A Celebration

of the World's Favorite Drink. New York: Skyhorse, 2013. Print.

Liu, Tong. Chinese Tea. United Kingdom: Cambridge University Press, 2012. Print.

Uhl, Joseph Wesley. The Art and Craft of Tea: An Enthusiast's Guide to Selecting, Brewing, and Serving Exquisite Tea. London: Quarry Books, 2015. Kindle edition.

By Title

茶之路。《生活月刊》編著。桂林：廣西師範大學出版社，2014（2015重印）。書籍。

評茶員培訓教材。楊亞軍（主編）。北京：金盾出版社，2009（2017重印）。書籍。

圖解茶經 [新版]。陸羽（原著）、蕭亦珊（主編）。台北：華威國際事業有限公司，2016。書籍。

The Story of Tea: A Cultural History and Drinking Guide. Mary Lou Heiss and Robert J. Heiss. Berkeley: Ten Speed Press, 2011. Kindle Edition.

Tea: History, Terroirs, Varieties. Kevin Gascoyne, Francois Marchand, Jasmine Desharnais and Hugo Americi. Ontario: Firefly Books, 2013. Print.

The Tea Enthusiast's Handbook: A Guide to the World's Best Teas. Mary Lou Heiss and Robert J. Heiss. Berkeley: Ten Speed Press, 2012. Kindle Edition.

INTERVIEWS

Chen Luho, Green Light Tea Farm (綠光農園)
www.facebook.com/chenluho

Jacob Bai, By Tea Master (白青長茶作坊)
www.by-teamaster.com

Liang Minjie, Ji Xi Tea Company (吉兮茶庄)

San Wen, Weng Ji Tea Company (翁基茶葉)

Zhu Jianying, Weng Jia Shan Tea Plantation

Wilson Hsu, Hsu Yaoliang Tea Co. LTD
(徐耀良茶園)
www.hoshiuantea.com

William Osmont, Farmerleaf
www.farmer-leaf.com

TEA PAIRING SUGGESTIONS

May Chan, Homeland Tea Garden
www.homelandteagarden.com

Ann Sit, Fook Ming Tong
www.fookmingtong.com

Catherine Yung, yú teahouse
www.yuteahouse.com

Nana Chan, PLANTATION Teas
www.plantation.hk

Copyright © 2025 Man Mo Media Limited
All rights reserved

Published in Hong Kong
Printed in Shenzhen (physical book)

1st Edition: September 2019
2nd Edition: February 2025

ISBN 978-988-77560-7-1

For more details about our company and/or our products (including EU compliance information), go to manmomedia.com or send an email to books@manmomedia.com.

Lead Author: Chan Sin Yan

Editor: Adele Wong

Creative Directors: Edmund Ip (1st Edition); Mike Hung (2nd Edition)

Photographers: Paul Leong, Cyrus Wong, Edwin Liem

No part of this publication may be reproduced, distributed, or transmitted in any form or by any means, including photocopying, recording, or other electronic or mechanical methods, without the prior written permission of the publisher, except in the case of brief quotations embodied in critical reviews and certain other non-commercial uses. For permission requests, write to the publisher at books@manmomedia.com.

Books should be disposed of and recycled according to local requirements. All paper materials used by our printer are FSC-compliant.

Our printers comply to international standards and local laws.

Books produced by us are not considered to be toys. However, based on information obtained from our ink, chemical and material suppliers, we can confirm that all of our inks, varnishes and additives would be safe to be used in the manufacture of toys. We hold documentation from all of our printers to confirm the above - Our printers comply with international standards and local laws.

ManMoMedia